# The King's Cross S

## 200 YEARS OF HISTORY IN THE RAILW...

### Peter Darley

The History Press

This book is dedicated to Käthe Strenitz.

Title page: East Handyside Canopy looking north, Käthe Strenitz, courtesy of Käthe Strenitz Estate. (LMA)

Right: A railway clearance auction at King's Cross Station, W.B. Murray (engr.), *The Graphic*, 1875. (SSPL/NRM)

First published 2018

Reprinted 2019

The History Press
The Mill, Brimscombe Port
Stroud, Gloucestershire, GL5 2QG
www.thehistorypress.co.uk

© Peter Darley, 2018

The right of Peter Darley to be identified as the Author of this work has been asserted in accordance with the Copyright, Designs and Patents Act 1988.

British Library Cataloguing in Publication Data.
A catalogue record for this book is available from the British Library.

ISBN 978 0 7509 8579 6

Typesetting and origination by The History Press
Printed and bound in India by Thomson Press India Ltd

**Camden Railway Heritage Trust (www.crht1837.org)**
Camden Railway Heritage Trust (CRHT) is a charity promoting, for public benefit, the preservation and restoration of the railway and associated heritage, access to the heritage and the education of the public in the broad appreciation of the social and industrial history of the area.

The author's revenue from the sale of this book goes to Camden Railway Heritage Trust.

# Contents

# Foreword

Few areas of the capital have changed as much in the past decades as the King's Cross Railway Lands. Even in the 1990s they were still largely unknown territory to most Londoners, visible in enigmatic glimpses from the streets around, or sliding inaccessibly past the windows of a moving train. What were all the hulking, apparently abandoned buildings for? And where were all those branching railway lines going?

Peter Darley's splendid book gives us the answers, and more besides. His account of the Great Northern Railway's celebrated terminus at King's Cross is merely the prelude to an exploration northward, taking in tunnels and viaducts, coal drops and canals, warehouses and workshops of every description.

It is a journey as much through time as through space. Structures vanish, change use, or are transformed by renovation. The mighty Granary Building of 1852 – lately reborn as the home of Central St Martins art college – turns out to have doubled for much of its life as a repository for Continental containers and sugar. Another former storage shed incorporates ironwork from the Great Northern's first temporary station. Suitably adapted, this relic of the summer before the Great Exhibition now sits within a very singular branch of Waitrose.

Darley is interested in why, as well as what and when. His account of the stables buildings opens up the story of London's working horses, right down to their posthumous transformation at the hands of knackers and glue-boilers. Economic factors and statistics are brought to life by showing what they meant in terms of work and experience. There is plenty to say about potatoes, and it is fascinating. The railway lands of King's Cross prove to be a mirror to London's working world.

In decline, the district fostered unconventional activities of many kinds, from notorious street prostitution to go-karting and raves. They find their place here too – even the unforgettable Mutoid Waste Company.

A special pleasure is the generous selection of drawings by the late Käthe Strenitz. At once bold and meticulous, they distil the mood of decline and abandonment that followed the end of steam. That time of eclipse has passed away in turn, as regeneration opens up the area. Many historic buildings have been lost, but what remains is accessible as never before.

Peter Darley did a great service to metropolitan history with his *Camden Goods Station Through Time* (Amberley Publishing, 2013), a deceptively plain title for a wonderfully rich treatment. His new book goes beyond even that high standard. It should be read by railway enthusiasts and lovers of London alike.

Simon Bradley

# Introduction

With the arrival of the Great Northern Railway, King's Cross connected 'the country' to London, supporting the need for goods and transport of the ever-growing metropolis. Limited by statute from approaching closer to the City than the New Road, the terminus was located on the Regent's Canal, promoting goods interchange between rail, road and canal networks and with the London Docks.

Before the arrival of the railway and under pressure from the expanding capital, the area had already started to be transformed from fields and market gardens, occasionally flooded by the River Fleet. This 'River of Wells' had once been synonymous with pleasure gardens for Londoners taking the waters. In their vicinity was established the Smallpox Hospital and terraces of simpler housing. Even less salubrious was the growth of tile kilns and dust heaps serving the need for building materials and for recycling waste.

King's Cross Railway Lands stretch loosely from the Euston Road in the south to beyond the North London Railway, and from Pancras Road in the west to York Way. They housed passenger stations, goods yards, coal yards, locomotive sheds, potato markets, stables and other infrastructure, as well as the associated rolling stock, attracting industry and commerce to the area.

This book's focus is on the hinterland to King's Cross Station, largely hidden from the public. It charts its growth during the nineteenth century, the competition for trade, the later consolidation, the weakness between the wars, the high age of steam, and the subsequent decline under pressure from road transport. It examines operations, the essential support role played by the horse, and how activities in the Railway Lands affected the neighbourhood.

The emphasis is on the goods yard and the infrastructure that ensured the supply of coal and commodities to the metropolis. As Simon Bradley (*The Railways*, 2016) expresses it: 'For those that have been initiated, a unique allure resides in the fabric and architecture of the railways, rather than in the trains themselves.'

After the demise of steam, the stark industrial landscape that was revealed after opening the Regent's Canal towpath inspired artists and photographers, and was colonised by a variety of small enterprises. Its potential for large-scale development became a battleground over which competing ideas for the future were fought.

In the new millennium, the Railway Lands have become an immense construction site. A world of glass and steel is rising above the rich historical features that represent one of the most important industrial heritage complexes in the country.

This book tells the story of the Railway Lands largely through images, and omits footnotes and references that would break the flow of the narrative. Those who would actively seek further substantiation are invited to comment, contribute, challenge and correct by contacting the author.

For those who live, work or pass through this unfolding panorama, or those interested in transport, railways or local history, this book provides the threads linking past and present, and shows how features have evolved through time and space. Above all, *The King's Cross Story* celebrates our industrial heritage.

Camden Railway Heritage Trust, www.CRHT1837.org

# Acknowledgements

My thanks to my editor, Amy Rigg, and her colleagues at The History Press, who have guided the book from its inception, and had to field the many challenges thrown up during its passage.

I acknowledge my debt of gratitude to Lucy Isenberg, and to the estate of Katerina Fischel (née Strenitz), which grants permission for the reproduction of the images in this book, and in future editions of the same. The right to reproduction is non-transferable. Thanks are also due to Jeremy Smith of London Metropolitan Archives, which holds the Käthe Strenitz drawings, for his help in making them available.

I am very grateful to three other artists – the late David Shepherd, Anne Howeson and Marianne Fox-Ockinga – for allowing me to use their work, which has strong resonance for the story.

Chimney of *Mallard*.
(SSPL/NRM)

Special thanks are due to Sue Elliott for providing the manuscript and typescript of Charlie Mayo's diaries, and to Rob Inglis for allowing me to use Angela Inglis' photographs and poems.

Both *King's Cross Voices* and the *LNER Discussion Forum* have proved rich sources of colour that have been mined for material.

I have borrowed freely from many books, particularly from Frank McKenna's greatly underrated book *The Railway Workers*. But the most remarkable is Pre-Construct Archaeology's *Monograph 1*, and I fully acknowledge the help received from Becky Haslam of P-CA, starting with a meeting at her offices in November 2015. This book was written before *Monographs 2* and *3* were published, and any future edition should benefit from these.

The help received with images is partly acknowledged in the credits, but this does not express my gratitude to all that have been so generous with their personal and corporate material, as well as with their time. A particular debt is owed to Michael Bussell, David Challis, Malcolm and Richard Holmes, Marian Kamlish, Peter Kay of London Railway Record, Brian Morrison, George Reeve of Irwell Press, Robert Thorne, Peter Townend, Malcolm Tucker, and Tim Watson of the Model Railway Club.

I have received enormous help with images from Argent, the asset manager for the King's Cross Central Limited Partnership that is redeveloping the site.

My thanks to my wife Edith for her tolerance of the demands of the book over the two years of its gestation, and her many suggestions for making the text and images more comprehensible.

While acknowledging the substantial help received from so many sources, the use of this material is entirely the author's responsibility, and any errors must be laid at his door.

Every care has been taken to trace copyright holders. Any that the author has been unable to reach are invited to contact the author via the publishers so that a full acknowledgement may be made in subsequent editions.

# Abbreviations

| | | | | |
|---|---|---|---|---|
| ARP | Air Raid Precautions | | KXRLG | King's Cross Railway Lands Group |
| ASLEF | Associated Society of Locomotive Engineers and Firemen | | LCR | London and Continental Railways |
| BR | British Railways | | LC&D | London Chatham and Dover Railway |
| C&D | Cartage and Delivery | | LMA | London Metropolitan Archives |
| CGM | Chief General Manager | | LMS | London Midland and Scottish Railway |
| CLSAC | Camden Local Studies and Archives Centre | | LNER | London and North Eastern Railway |
| CRT | Canal and River Trust | | LNWR | London and North Western Railway |
| CSM | Central St Martins, University of the Arts | | L&Y | London and York Railway |
| | | | MR | Midland Railway |
| CSNP | Camley Street Natural Park | | MRC | Model Railway Club |
| CTRL | Channel Tunnel Rail Link | | NA | National Archives |
| DfT | Department for Transport | | NCL | National Carriers Limited |
| ECML | East Coast Main Line | | NFC | National Freight Corporation/ Consortium |
| GLC | Greater London Council | | | |
| GLIAS | Greater London Industrial Archaeology Society | | NLR | North London Railway |
| | | | NRM | National Railway Museum |
| GM | General Manager | | NUR | National Union of Railwaymen |
| GN | Great Northern | | OD | Ordnance Datum |
| GNR | Great Northern Railway | | OS | Ordnance Survey |
| GWR | Great Western Railway | | P-CA | Pre-Construct Archaeology |
| HST | High Speed Train | | SC | Select Committee |
| ICE | Institution of Civil Engineers | | SSPL | Science and Society Picture Library |
| ILN | *Illustrated London News* | | TUC | Trades Union Congress |
| ILHC | Islington Local History Centre | | V&A | Victoria and Albert Museum |
| KCCLP | King's Cross Central Limited Partnership | | WCML | West Coast Main Line |

# A Sunday Stroll up Maiden Lane

# one

## THE COACHING INN

Our story starts with a visitor from the north who has come to London on business in the 1830s and is staying at the George and Blue Boar Inn in High Holborn (1.1). The journey of 384 miles (616km) to Edinburgh was now just three days with twenty-seven post stops to change horses. Coaches drawn by four horses left from the George and Blue Boar every night at 10.30 p.m. and stopped for the night only at Newcastle, averaging 7mph (11km/h), including stops for refreshment.

1.1: The George and Blue Boar Inn at 270 High Holborn, coachyard, April 1837. A medieval inn, it was one of many coaching inns in that area. In the city alone there were about twenty-five famous houses, many renowned for their accommodation for travellers. The inn was demolished in 1864. (CLSAC)

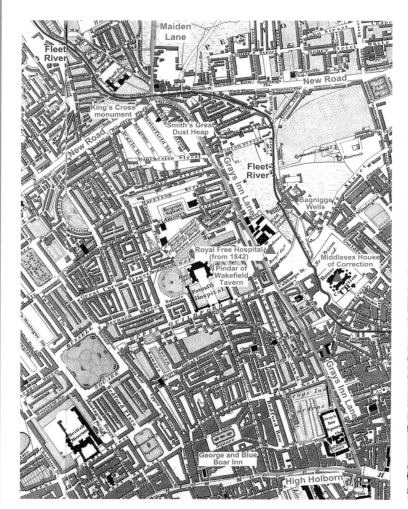

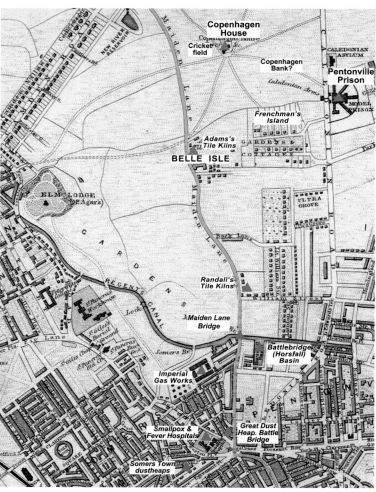

Above left: **1.2**: High Holborn to Battle Bridge, extract from Greenwood's map of 1827.

Above right: **1.3**: Battle Bridge to Copenhagen House, extract from Davies' map of 1843.

The George and Blue Boar was infamous as a stop-off en route from the East End to the hangings at Tyburn (Marble Arch). The convict would be escorted into the inn for a last drink, and the innkeeper would dispense it with a 'pay me on the way back', immortalised by Jonathan Swift, author of *Gulliver's Travels*, in his 1727 poem *Clever Tom Clinch*:

As clever Tom Clinch, while the rabble was bawling
Rode stately through Holborn to die in his calling.
He stopped at The George for a bottle of sack
And promised to pay for it when he came back.

But in the 1830s things were changing rapidly. Discussion at the inn was dominated by the railways. The London and Greenwich Railway Company had floated in 1831, and others were in the wings, laying bills before Parliament, notably the London & Birmingham Railway, which in 1832 was planning a London terminus at Battle Bridge off Maiden Lane. Their anticipated arrival represented a major threat to the coaching business.

Our visitor decides that he will spend his Sunday exploring the fringes of the metropolis, where the railways would locate their termini, before taking the coach back north. His destination would be Copenhagen House, a comfortable stroll of 2½ miles (4km) that will take about an hour, offering exercise, refreshments and views of the City and its surroundings, a Sunday purpose shared with many Londoners. His route is shown on maps 1.2 and 1.3.

## HOLBORN TO BATTLE BRIDGE VIA GRAY'S INN LANE

From the north side of High Holborn, he walks east and turns north up Gray's Inn Lane. He passes Coldbath Fields Debtors' Prison (Middlesex House of Correction), perched on a mound above the marshy areas along the River Fleet. Coldbath Fields' grim reputation was reinforced by the regime of hard labour introduced in the early 1820s. Central to this regime was the treadwheel, the first being installed in 1822 to designs by its inventor William Cubitt, later the Great Northern Railway's Consulting Engineer.

**1.4**: Bagnigge Wells Road (now King's Cross Road) from the Northumberland Arms around 1810, looking south along the River Fleet. This painting was commissioned by Randall, whose pre-1828 tile kilns are on the east side of the road. Behind the tree are Bagnigge Wells Gardens, which opened in 1759 and closed in 1841. The River Fleet was here diverted into a sewer in 1825, the low lying marshy ground in the foreground being prone to flooding. The turreted building beyond the tile kilns is Coldbath Fields Prison, while the building on higher ground on the right is the Foundling Hospital. (London Metropolitan Archives, City of London)

A little further lies Bagnigge Wells and its tearooms and gardens on the banks of the Fleet (1.4), its reputation long in decline. Our visitor notes how the growing metropolis is extending its tentacles into the surrounding fields, many of which have been stripped for brick earth and are now being laid out for residential development.

## BATTLE BRIDGE AND RIVER FLEET

At Battle Bridge the River Fleet crossed the dust fields owned by John Smith. Here amid the brickworks stood the 'Great Dust Heap', located where the New Road joined Gray's Inn Lane. The enormous hill of ashes stacked at the north end of Gray's Inn Lane in Battle Bridge Field had accumulated for many years, providing coal ash to be mixed with brick earth. The fine quality and great depth of the brick earth locally has been confirmed by recent excavations for blocks of flats on the nearby estate.

**1.5**: Battle Bridge, 1814, view south from Maiden Lane down Gray's Inn Lane with the New Road crossing from the left. The building on the corner, the White Hart public house, has striking similarities to the Lighthouse building that is there now. (Wellcome Collection)

THE KING'S CROSS STORY: 200 YEARS OF HISTORY IN THE RAILWAY LANDS

According to the Survey of London, Smith's Great Dust Heap was removed in 1826 when the ground was sold to the Panharmonium Company. In his *History of Clerkenwell*, William J. Pinks asserted that the dust heap was sold by W.F. Bray, the builder of Derby Street, to the Emperor of Russia for a large sum (£20,000 is mentioned by others) to help rebuild Moscow after Napoleon's invasion and its destruction by fire in 1812. This improbable legend appears to have extended to a second successor dust heap, just a stone's throw away (1.8).

The Fleet, a river that had been navigable in earlier times, marked the ancient route from Holborn up Gray's Inn Lane and St Pancras Way to the north. Gray's Inn Lane, the New Road, St Pancras Way and Maiden Lane all converged on Battle Bridge, for a long time a transport hub where a broad ford crossed the River Fleet. St Pancras Way is still the continuation of what is now Gray's Inn Road to Kentish Town, following the former bank of the River Fleet. Flooding of the low-lying areas around the marshes of St Pancras caused those that could afford it to move to higher ground at Kentish Town, Highgate and Hampstead.

The name Battle Bridge was attached not only to the hamlet near the ancient bridge (1.5), but also to the fields to the south on both sides of Gray's Inn Lane. A chapel was built near the south end of Maiden Lane in the 1770s and a few small houses existed by the end of the century, inhabited mainly by shopkeepers, artisans and labourers in 1810. The area was made unattractive by its proximity to the Fleet and the trades that had gathered there, including a pottery, a paint manufacturer and a bone collector.

The Battle Bridge area developed an early reputation for crime, even in Elizabethan times, when Old St Pancras Church was:

Visited by thieves, who assemble not there to pray, but to wait for praye, and manie fall into their hands clothed, that are glad when they escape naked. Walk there not too late … (Norden, 1593)

… The chief nurserys of all these evil people is fields of Pancrass and about the Churche, the Brick kylnes near Islyngton, and the Wells [letter to Elizabeth I].

Later, Fagin in *Oliver Twist* instructs his new charges in 'the kinchin lay':

'The kinchins, my dear,' said Fagin, 'is the young children that's sent on errands by their mothers, with sixpences and shillings; and the lay is just to take their money away …'

'… And you can have a few good beats chalked out in Camden Town, and Battle Bridge, and neighbourhoods like that, where they're always going errands, and you can upset as many kinchins as you want, any hour in the day. Ha! ha! ha!'

In 1755, influential residents of St Marylebone, Paddington and Islington – all separate villages close to London – petitioned Parliament for the right to provide a turnpike trust road bypassing the northern boundaries of the built-up area of London. The New Road from Paddington to Islington was built in

Above left: **1.6**: Monument to George IV, Battle Bridge, 1835, George Sidney Shepherd. (LMA)

Above right: **1.7**: The Inoculating Hospital, or Smallpox Hospital, with Fever Hospital on the left, George Sidney Shepherd. (Wellcome Collection)

1756 to connect Paddington, now the terminus of the Grand Junction Canal, with the City via Battle Bridge and Pentonville. It was intended initially as a drovers' road, a route along which to drive cattle and sheep to the live meat market at Smithfield from roads approaching London from the north and north-west, thereby avoiding the congested east–west route via Oxford Street and High Holborn.

In 1829 the first horse omnibus ('for all' in Latin) service in London was established by George Shillibeer. His example was followed by many others, and the New Road became the main artery for such traffic for the remainder of the century, linking the sought-after north-western suburbs of 'Tyburnia' (between Praed Street and the Bayswater Road) with the City. By the 1830s, much of the road was bordered by fashionable houses.

To raise the reputation of Battle Bridge, in 1835 Stephen Geary (the architect of Highgate Cemetery) erected a monument to George IV and, rather pretentiously, called the site 'King's Cross' (1.6). The monument itself was crowned with a statue of the king that attracted derision from passers-by, who recalled an unpopular and indulgent 20-stone monarch. The building below had been used as place of exhibition, police station and finally beer shop until, in 1842, the St Pancras Vestry ordered the statue of the king to be pulled down as it was a nuisance to traffic.

## SMALLPOX HOSPITAL

Picking his way across the New Road to avoid the ordure hazards, our traveller observes the avenue that leads to the Smallpox and Fever Hospitals (1.7). Known variously as the London Smallpox Hospital and the Middlesex County Hospital for Smallpox, this charitable institution was established in 1745–46, originally in Windmill Street. The hospital's association with St Pancras began in 1763 when a house was purchased for inoculations. This house was replaced by a new building erected at St Pancras. Opened in 1767, the hospital had about 100 beds and was supported mainly by voluntary contributions; it was intended for paying patients but would take paupers if beds were available. It was one of only two isolation hospitals in London. A separate Smallpox Hospital was built alongside in 1793–94, and the London Fever Hospital was built in 1801 a little to the west.

Both buildings were demolished in 1850 to make way for the GNR terminus (now King's Cross Station). The Fever Hospital moved to a new building in Islington, in Liverpool Road, while the Smallpox Hospital moved to Highgate Hill, on the site of the present Whittington Hospital.

## DUST HEAPS

The site of the future GNR terminus, immediately north of the New Road and west of Maiden Lane, was also occupied by dust heaps and streets of small terraced houses (1.8).

At this time the parish employed private contractors to remove dust. Householders were forever lodging complaints against the dustmen, who were seldom to be found when needed and had their own way of letting it be known that their services were not free. The dry dust would get into their

Below left: **1.8**: View of the Great Dustheap, King's Cross, Battle Bridge, 1837, from the Maiden Lane, painted by E.H. Dixon. A later painting by Dixon from 1840 shows the same scene in winter and the annotation refers to Mr Starkey as the owner of the Great Dustheap. Note the tower of the Smallpox Hospital on the extreme right. (Wellcome Collection)

Below right: **1.9**: Dust heaps, Somers Town, 1836. The large building with the domed tower is the Smallpox Hospital. Tile kilns are seen in the right distance, from the same general area around Battle Bridge. (Wellcome Collection)

throats and cause an abnormal thirst that could only be allayed by copious quantities of beer, or by a few pence to purchase the needed antidote. This sort of blackmail was not unfamiliar even quite recently.

Somers Town became a dense shanty town, surrounded on several sides by brickfields and dust heaps (1.9).

Dust yards were often located near to a river or canal, chosen because a large quantity of dust and ashes was taken by sailing barges to Faversham, Sittingbourne and other places in Kent where there were large brick-making fields.

The largest heap of 'soil' (the finer portion of the dust), was placed near the centre of the dust yard. Around it, several smaller heaps would be waiting to be sifted.

In the first half of the nineteenth century, dust had a high value. It provided:

* fine dust used in making bricks
* fine dust as soil conditioner, rendering marshy soil fit for cultivation
* coarse dust or 'breeze' used in burning bricks
* bones, used for making buttons and other articles
* fragments of tin and other metals used to reinforce the corners of trunks
* old boots and shoes for London bootmakers to use as stuffing
* rags and paper to be recycled for paper
* 'core' (broken crockery, bricks, oyster shells, broken bottles) for road foundation.

Maiden Lane had long been associated with brick fields and tile kilns, and these would have been associated with the dust or midden heaps from which Maiden Lane derived its name.

While dustmen and cinder-sifters were widely considered the pariahs of the metropolis, Dickens in *Our Mutual Friend* described the female labourers at Mr Dodds' dust yard, 1¼ miles up Maiden Lane, as 'fat, rosy and laughing, and among the healthiest of our working population'.

## IMPERIAL GAS LIGHT AND COKE COMPANY

Our traveller continues northwards up the gentle rise that is Maiden Lane. It marked the parish boundary between St Pancras and Islington. The ancient boundaries of fields and tracks would be largely preserved when developed later in the nineteenth century. Goods Way still follows an early shortcut from Maiden Lane to Pancras Way.

Approaching Regent's Canal, he observes on the left the works of the Imperial Gas Light and Coke Company with its twin chimneys (1.10), his nostrils filling with the sulphurous odours carried on the westerly breeze.

In 1821 negotiations opened with the Governors of St Bartholomew's Hospital for purchase of the land, and with the Regent's Canal Company for the opening of an 'Indent' for the unloading of coal from barges.

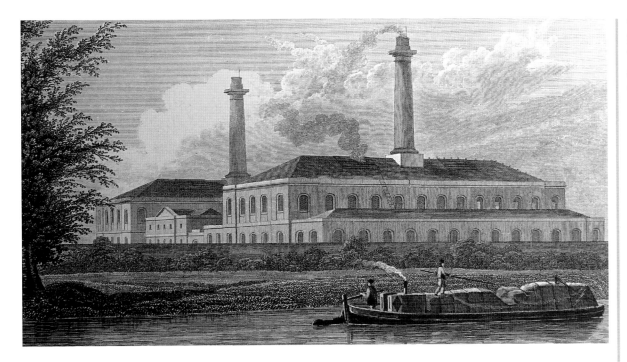

**1.10**: Gas Works, near the Regent's Canal, May 1828, T.H. Shepherd. The serene appearance belies the frenetic activity behind. (Alan Faulkner collection)

The gasworks opened in August 1824, the site covering 11 acres. It was claimed to be the largest and finest in the world.

The gas was produced in retorts, fire-clay ovens heated by coke furnaces placed beneath them. After coal had been fed into the retort, the airtight door was closed, and gas was then driven up ascension pipes. When all the gas had been extracted, coke was drawn out by a rake. A ton of coal yielded 10,000 cu. ft ($283m^3$) of gas, about 10 gallons (45l) of tar, 12 gallons (55l) of ammonia-water and 13 to 14 cwt (660–710kg) of coke.

## REGENT'S CANAL

The view north from Maiden Lane bridge in 1835 (1.11) shows fields and market gardens stretching up to Holloway, with a large mansion, Copenhagen House, on the crest of the hill. The land slopes east to west down to the River Fleet.

The property boundary of Counsellor Agar, who fought protracted legal battles with the Regent's Canal Company over the canal alignment, is clearly marked by the wood. It includes a parcel of land that can be reached via Somers Bridge (a little further to the west), rural tracks connecting this parcel with Elm Lodge, his mansion.

Above left: **1.11**: A view of Maiden Lane, 1835, E.H. Dixon. (ILHC)

Above right: **1.12**: Randall's tile kilns, King's Cross, looking north-east towards Islington in 1832, George Sidney Shepherd. The view is from close to where Shepherd grew up. The figures in the foreground have dug clay for making bricks and are filling a clay pit, while the horse is puddling the clay/water mix before it is fired in the kiln behind. Recently fired bricks can be seen stacked in the doorway of the wooden hut. (V&A)

But the features are not all rural: large areas had been let for brickmaking from 1808. The first track off Maiden Lane to the east was William Street, now Copenhagen Street. Beyond that lies the nearer pair of tile kilns, Randall's kilns, which moved from Battle Bridge in 1828 as London expanded. The northern pair of tile kilns, Adams' kilns, is at Belle Isle, where modern day Tileyard Road (formerly Tile Kilns Road) recalls their presence. Between the two pairs of kilns and their associated settlements of houses, can be seen the '4 acre field' that is being excavated to extract brick earth and clay for brick and tile making.

He crosses Regent's Canal. The canal opened on 1 August 1820, finally connecting the Grand Junction Canal at Paddington with the London Docks at Limehouse. The committee and shareholders marked the occasion by embarking on the ceremonial barge at Horsfall's Basin (now Battlebridge Basin), immediately to the east of the bridge. Only then was the world's greatest port linked to the eighteenth-century canal network that connected with England's industrial heartlands.

In 1835 one-fifth of all coal imported into London entered the canal, mostly for local use. The traffic of goods from the north and from the London Docks – coal, iron, timber, beer and ice – saw a rapid development of industry and warehousing at Horsfall's Basin, and this spread to neighbouring streets.

## BRICK FIELDS AND TILE KILNS

With the opening of the canal, industry was already competing to spread into the nearby fields. Small settlements had grown up on the east side of Maiden Lane based on brickmaking, in parts of what is now Barnsbury, as early as Elizabethan times. Stone was always expensive in London as it had to be imported from a distance, but wooden buildings had been outlawed since the Great Fire: this massively

**1.13**: Belle Isle, view to the west in about 1835, E.H. Dixon. The Fortune of War public house is on the right; a later version was built in the same location, 184 York Road. St Pancras Old Church can be seen in the distance, and to the north of it is what must be St Pancras Workhouse, now St Pancras Hospital. (LMA)

**1.14**: Frenchman's Island or Experimental Gardens *c*.1845. The view over Belle Isle to Primrose Hill. (LMA)

**1.15**: Approaching Copenhagen House from Frenchman's Island, July 1841, E.H. Dixon. (LMA)

**1.16**: Copenhagen House, *c*.1815. (ILHC)

increased the demand for bricks. The rapid growth of the city placed a heavy demand on building materials. Fortunately, London had suitable clay in abundance. The Thames flood plain is overlain by a geological formation known generally as 'brick earth', and this material, rather than the intractable London clay, provided the basis for the ubiquitous stock brick from which much of Victorian London was built. Brick earth seams were shallow, no more than 5–6ft (1.5–1.8m) deep, and therefore were quickly exhausted.

Brick manufacture involved digging up fields for the brick earth beneath and then firing the slabs in tall, purpose-built kilns (1.12). These structures rose dramatically against the skyline, attracting artists but polluting the environment. The area around Battle Bridge and north to Belle Isle was conveniently close to the City but far enough away for land to be cheaper and the environmental degradation less evident. It was ideal for brick and tile manufacture until nearby residential development made these activities increasingly unpopular.

Workmen in the brickmaking trade invariably worked by the piece, labouring sometimes from three in the morning until nine at night in the height of summer. They could earn extravagant wages, sometimes three or four guineas a week, which they would spend just as extravagantly in one of the many local public houses. They were often reduced to dismal straits in the winter, when they could not work.

## BELLE ISLE AND FRENCHMAN'S ISLAND

In marked contrast to its name, Belle Isle (1.13) was an industrial slum, principally known for its horse-slaughterer, John Atcheler, but also the establishment of noxious industries such as the making of cart grease and varnish. Adams, who made chimney pots and garden pots, had a large kiln there, as well as a smaller one that was used as a store, sheds and cottages.

West of the Caledonian Road, the tile kilns and pollution from industries at Belle Isle exasperated householders who had moved to the area for fresh air, and caused a rapid decline in its desirability.

Between Belle Isle and Caledonian Road, three or four streets formed Experimental Gardens, also known as Frenchman's Colony or Island (1.14). The settlement had been established in 1837 by Pierre Henri Joseph Baume, a philanthropist, who had intended it as a community formed on the principles of Robert Owen.

Robert Owen was an enlightened mill owner who set up shops for his workers on the cooperative principle, passing on the savings from bulk purchase. He proposed subordinating the machine to the united action of men in communities of about 1,200, a size similar to that at his renowned mill at New Lanark where he operated and called for an eight-hour day. Children older than three would be brought up by the community, anticipating later arrangements introduced in kibbutzim.

Baume let small plots on which poor people could build, and he himself built cottages for sale or letting. Missionaries opened a school in a cottage there in 1839 with Sunday services, to counteract the influence of the 'infidel Frenchman'; the services soon failed but the school had about seventy children in 1846. On Sundays, the colony attracted passers-by with its swings and roundabouts.

Due to poor lighting and roads, the cottages declined into slums and developed a fearsome reputation as a rookery, parallel to that of Agar Town. Such a reputation commonly had elements of resentment of working-class independence, a freedom secretly envied by many of the middle class. This cultural divide grew wider when working-class areas developed a vocabulary from nineteenth-century thieves' and costers' slang that was often unintelligible to those in neighbouring streets.

## COPENHAGEN HOUSE

Continuing a little way, our traveller reaches the path leading off Maiden Lane to Copenhagen House (1.15). The road ahead leads up to Holloway and Highgate. Not far west, over lands owned by St Bartholomew's Hospital, where once were the pleasure grounds of the River of Wells, he observes the landscape starting to be filled by new modest dwellings.

Copenhagen House (1.16) had a small garden with seats and tables. It was a licensed tavern as well as a tea garden with outdoor entertainments. Surrounded by fields that were used by Sunday strollers, it had become one of the pleasure resorts of north London, with commanding views of the city below and up to the heights of Hampstead and Highgate. It was one of several questionable houses of entertainment that Londoners could visit for a day out. Our traveller decides to halt his journey for some refreshment.

The landlady had been encouraged to build a fives court and the first ball used in play was made there. Based on an ancient form of handball, this was the start of a sport for which Copenhagen House became famous, and it appears to have predated both Rugby and Eton fives. There was also a well-arranged ground for cricket and other healthy amusements.

## COPENHAGEN FIELDS

In the late eighteenth century Copenhagen Fields became a popular venue for radical demonstrations. In 1795, two such protests were attended by crowds of over 100,000 people, and one was followed by rioting in central London.

On 21 April 1834, 50–60,000 members of the Trades' Union met in Copenhagen Fields (1.17) to convey a petition to His Majesty, asking for the repeal of the deportation sentence passed on six agricultural labourers who were also Dorchester unionists. These Dorchester labourers were neither the first nor the last trade unionists to be deported, but they created a focus for class conflict.

The Industrial Revolution had fostered a new social order, based on the horizontal union of wage earners rather than the vertical integration of trades. This new world of labour was progressive in outlook, democratic in spirit and egalitarian in ethos; it drew on the French Revolution and the Chartist movement. The new working class came to feel an identity of interest that was in direct opposition to their rulers and employers, while the propertied classes were haunted by the spectre of revolution, particularly in the five years leading up to 1834.

**1.17**: The grand meeting of the Metropolitan Trades' Unions at Copenhagen Fields, 21 April 1834. (LMA)

The events of 1834 may have passed relatively peaceably, but they continued to be invested with a special meaning by those seeking to uphold the rights of association. This culminated in the TUC's centenary celebrations in 1934, which canonised the Dorchester labourers as the Tolpuddle Martyrs.

# The London Station of the Great Northern Railway

## THE COMPANY AND ITS STRUCTURE

The extent of the London and York (L&Y) undertaking, as submitted to Parliament, dwarfed that of any railway project before or since, with 186 miles of main line and 142 miles of loop and branch lines.

A total of 224 railway bills were placed before Parliament in the 1844 session; the years between 1844 and 1846 were known as years of railway mania. There was strong and underhand competition for the east coast line between the major conurbations of London and Yorkshire, notably from the 'Railway King', George Hudson. The bill went into a further parliamentary session, 562 railway bills being submitted to the House of Commons in 1845. With much political wrangling, the passage of the bill degenerated into the longest parliamentary contest on record. Legal fees amounted to over half a million pounds, an enormous sum at that time.

On 30 May 1846, the name of the company was changed to Great Northern Railway (GNR) after the Great Northern amalgamated with the L&Y. Royal assent was then obtained on 26 June 1846, with the company capitalised at £5.6 million.

The GN directors met for the first time at No. 36 Great George Street, Westminster on 1 July 1846 and confirmed William Cubitt's appointment as Consulting Engineer (2.1). His son, Joseph Cubitt, was appointed Engineer for the southern portion of the works at a salary of £2,000 per annum.

In July 1846 the company offices were moved to No. 14 Moorgate, where they remained until 15 August 1850 when they were transferred to the temporary Maiden Lane Station.

William Cubitt recommended his brother Benjamin as Locomotive Engineer, and he was engaged on 3 November 1846 at a salary of £750 per annum, but died little more than a year later. He was succeeded by Edward Bury, a highly experienced locomotive engineer and manufacturer who took up the positions both of General Manager and Locomotive Engineer in February 1847. He resigned from both three years later, owing to conflicts of interest. Archibald Sturrock was appointed Locomotive Engineer in March 1850; Seymour Clarke was appointed General Manager in May 1850.

**2.1**: Sir William Cubitt's portrait hanging on main staircase at Institution of Civil Engineers, of which he was president from 1849–51. He was knighted for his role as one of the Commissioners of The Great Exhibition. (ICE)

Lewis Cubitt was appointed architect in December 1849 for the London Temporary Passenger Station and the permanent Goods Station. Any family connection with William and Joseph appears doubtful.

## THE TERMINUS SITE

King's Cross, where several key roads converged, was an obvious location for the main passenger station. When, in 1846, a Royal Commission recommended that no railway should be allowed further into London than the New Road, this effectively formed the southern boundary of the site.

To the east and west respectively, Maiden Lane and St Pancras Way, as major routes to the north, formed clear man-made boundaries. The northern boundary was to be formed by the planned East and West India Docks and Birmingham Junction Railway, which became the North London Railway (NLR) in 1853.

The Regent's Canal approached this area from the north-west, skirting William Agar's estate before turning east to cross the area. It thereby created a division between the goods station to the north, on the left bank of the canal, and the intended passenger station to the south, on the right bank of the canal. As well as providing access to the London Docks at Limehouse, the complex of canal/rail/road infrastructure created a major opportunity for goods interchange between transport modes.

Within these boundaries, the GNR purchased 40 acres (16 ha) of land for the goods yard from St Bartholomew's Hospital in May 1847. Land for the passenger station required the demolition of several streets of modest housing as well as the purchase and demolition of the Smallpox and Fever Hospitals, as seen in the 1846 plan submitted with the bill (2.2). The breakdown of negotiations for the hospital sites in October 1846 created the need for a temporary passenger terminus at Maiden Lane. Constructed north of the canal, this station was to be capable of being used for two to three years '... till such time as events may show whether it will be best to go down to King's Cross or complete the station permanently above the Canal' (William Cubitt to Board, 31 May 1849).

Both goods and passenger stations required land that was essentially level. The terrain chosen sloped gently from north to south and from east to west, at about 1 in 60 in both directions. Landform relates closely to the former course of the Fleet River, which drained the area (see 1.11, page 18).

A key decision, dictated by the proximity of the canal to the station, was to take the main line out of King's Cross main passenger station under the Regent's Canal, which was to be carried over the railway in a cast-iron aqueduct formed of plates 1½in (38mm) thick. A departing train was to be given an impetus by an initial descent at 1 in 100 to a point below the canal aqueduct in order to gain sufficient speed for the ascent to the top of the Northern Heights at Holloway. William Cubitt tolerated a rise of 1 in 108 from the aqueduct to level ground at Holloway, in contrast with a maximum ruling gradient of 1 in 200 over the rest of the line.

Entirely different solutions were adopted at Euston and St Pancras stations. The London & Birmingham Railway faced a steeper incline from Euston to Camden up to the Regent's Canal Bridge, and so opted to draw trains up the Camden Incline by a stationary engine. At St Pancras, the Midland Railway raised the terminus on vaults to avoid such a steep gradient. This diversity of Victorian railway engineering can be appreciated by rail passengers to this day.

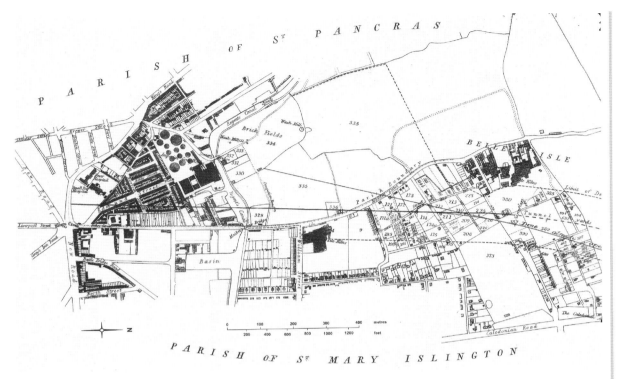

**2.2**: An extract from the Parliamentary Plan of 1846. (Parliamentary Archives HL/PO/PB/3/plan1846N56)

## CONSTRUCTION

Construction of the southernmost section of the GNR, let to the contractor John Jay in 1848, was held up by the Company not having full possession of the site. Negotiations to purchase the Smallpox and Fever hospitals broke down owing to a disparity between the GN's valuation of the site and the hospital owners' demands. Only in May 1850, after placing the dispute before a jury, could instructions be given to pull down the hospitals and sell the materials without delay.

Spoil from construction of the main passenger station was trucked over the canal to a tipping area on the goods yard site with the aid of an elevated wagonway (2.3). The wagonway can be identified outside the departure side of the Temporary Passenger Station (2.7), where it must have provided a ramshackle platform for the throng that had assembled to cheer the royal family. It therefore ran between the Carriage Shed (later the Midland Goods Shed) and the Departure Shed. The buildings and structures seen in the goods yard in 2.3 bear only passing resemblance to what was built.

A level terrace at approximately 24.2m OD was created for the main goods yard (the area shown in 2.4) some 3m above natural ground level, which is close to the towpath level at the Regent's Canal

along its southern and western boundaries. This can be observed in the height of the retaining walls along this section of the Regent's Canal (7.11, page 91). Other areas of the goods yard site were at a higher level, typically 25–26m OD, rising to 27.5m OD near the northern boundary. Northern and eastern areas of the site were excavated to fill areas in the south and west, leaving a slight fall from west to east. Some of this fill will have come from excavations for the main passenger station and from Gasworks and Copenhagen Tunnels. Most of the far northern area of the goods yard, between the locomotive shed and the NLR, remained undeveloped at this stage.

Work on Gasworks Tunnel started in October 1849 by 'cut and cover' rather than bored tunnel (unlike the two later tunnels, one each side of the first).

John Jay fired some of the excavated clay to create a granular permeable layer that provided a working surface over the newly levelled ground, avoiding conditions that could otherwise have resembled a First World War battlefield. In early 1850, Joseph Cubitt noted that almost 15 acres (6ha) had been dressed off to formation level, and that 30,000 cubic yards (23,000m$^3$) of 'good burnt clay ballast' was ready to be spread across the site. This implies an average depth of 1¼ft (0.38m) and ties in with recent archaeological investigations that found 'an orange layer of small burnt clay nodules, no more than 0.65m thick, above the redeposited London Clay' (Haslam, 2016).

## TEMPORARY PASSENGER STATION AND GOODS SHED

Lewis Cubitt's drawings of the goods yard and temporary passenger station, dated 30 March 1850, are held at the Institution of Civil Engineers (ICE). Drawing 1 and a part of Drawing 2 showing the Temporary Passenger Station are reproduced in 2.4 and 2.5. The plan shows five tunnels for barges to enter the Granary and Transit Sheds from the Dock or Basin and stabling in each of the Transit Sheds. Roofing of the Train Assembly Shed was 50 per cent complete; the remaining two bays were to be roofed within six months. These features are described in Chapter 4.

**2.4**: GNR London Terminus, Drawing 1, Plan Showing Sites of Iron Roofing. (ICE)

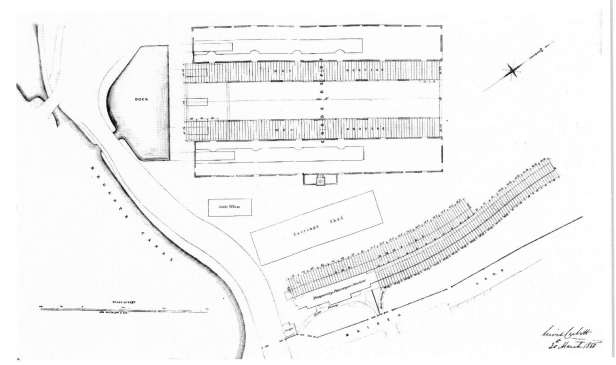

**2.5**: An extract from GNR London Terminus, Drawing 2: Transverse Sections of Iron Roofs, looking northwards, Section of Portion of Passenger Platform. (ICE)

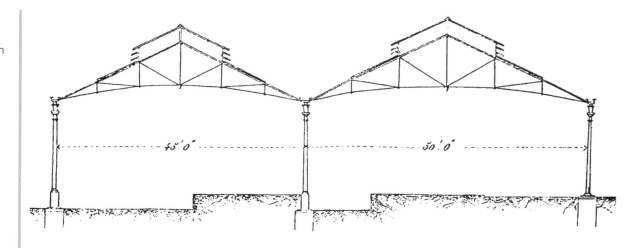

The Arrival Shed was closer to Maiden Lane and allowed passengers to board road vehicles under cover. Departing passengers would be dropped off at the Temporary Passenger Station, from where they could make their way through the station via the booking offices and waiting rooms to the Departure Shed.

The transverse section (2.5) shows the Departure Shed (left) with space for two tracks beyond the 20ft (6m) platform and the Arrival Shed with a single track, a similar width platform and an 18ft (5.5m) roadway under the roof. Both Arrival and Departure Sheds were built 475ft (145m) in length.

The Carriage Shed was designed to hold eighty carriages, and was to be 'of materials that will permit its removal elsewhere' (Joseph Cubitt to Board, 27 September 1849).

The line between the Temporary Passenger Station at King's Cross and Peterborough opened in August 1850. Very soon after opening, a northward extension was added to the east side of the Arrival Shed, 100ft (30.5m) long, under a third ridged roof. Its purpose remains speculative, but it could have provided for the loading/unloading of road carriages and horses, as suggested by the Duke of Wellington's experience described on page 30.

## GREAT EXHIBITION

The decision to provide a temporary passenger station was driven by the need to capture traffic for the Great Exhibition, an international exhibition that took place in the Crystal Palace in Hyde Park from 1 May to 15 October 1851.

Six million people (equivalent to a third of the entire population of Britain at the time) visited the Great Exhibition. The average daily attendance was 42,831, with a peak attendance of 109,915 on

By the 1840s, Edward Dent had established an international reputation as a watchmaker. On a visit to Russia in 1843, he was presented with a gold medal by order of the emperor for the services of his chronometers to that country.

In the same year he was selected to construct a clock for the rebuilt Royal Exchange. The works he established soon made such improvements to clockmaking that English clocks could compete with those of French manufacture. In 1852 he was entrusted with the order for the great clock at the new palace of Westminster, but did not live to see its construction, which was undertaken by his stepson and business partner, Frederick Dent.

7 October. The event made a surplus of £186,000 – this was used to found the Victoria and Albert Museum, the Science Museum and the Natural History Museum. The GNR used the exhibition to promote its services, and low fares stimulated a high and irregular volume of passenger traffic that proved difficult to manage.

Central to the exhibits in the British Avenue at the Crystal Palace was Dent's Turret Clock, which was awarded the Council Medal for its strength, accuracy and lower cost. It stood in the centre of the British Avenue and excited much attention (2.6).

The son of Edmund Denison, the chairman, when attending the exhibition was struck by the suitability of Dent's clock for use in the tower at King's Cross, and negotiated a price of £200 exclusive of three new dials. In 1853, Dent supplied a double-faced clock for the departure platform.

Above left: **2.6**: *Great Exhibition: Dent's Turret Clock, The Illustrated Exhibitor* of 1851. (Robert Thorne Collection)

Above right: **2.8**: 'The *Iron Duke* rides the Iron Road in 1852', *Railway Magazine*, VI, 1900. (ICE)

## EARLY TRAVELLERS

Queen Victoria's departure to Scotland from the arrival side of the GNR terminus at King's Cross on 27 August 1851 (2.7) is the only existing representation of the temporary terminus. It confirms what had been described as a light and elegant iron roof. In the far background a North London Railway train is seen. The public viewing platform seen on the left, just beyond the Departure side, appears to have been created from the temporary works that carried spoil from the permanent station site (2.3).

Archibald Sturrock, Locomotive Engineer of the GNR, was the driver of the royal train. The spandrels on the west side of the Departure-side roof are all that now survives of the temporary station (see 16.20).

While Queen Victoria had her own carriage, and a train for her entourage, others could also avoid the company of members of the public by paying for the rail transport of their carriage and horses. This was how the Duke of Wellington embarked on the GNR from the temporary station, a few months before his death on 14 September 1852. His carriage was rolled onto an open carriage truck, only partly protected from the elements (2.8), suggesting how strongly averse he was to sharing a railway carriage.

**2.7**: Queen Victoria and Prince Albert embark for Scotland from the Arrival Shed, Maiden Lane, ILN, 30 August 1851. (SSPL/NRM)

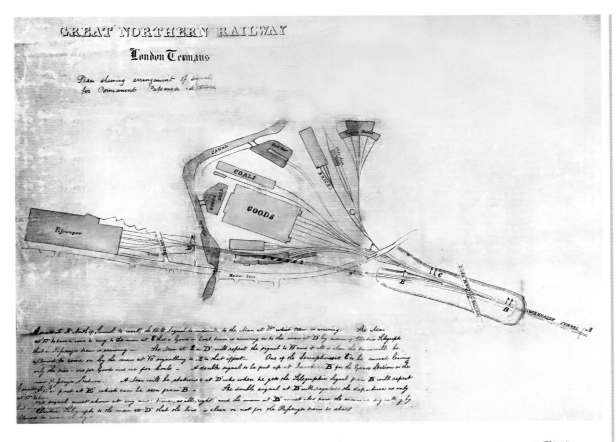

**2.9**: A plan by Captain Galton, showing arrangement of signals for permanent passenger station, October 1852. (National Archives)

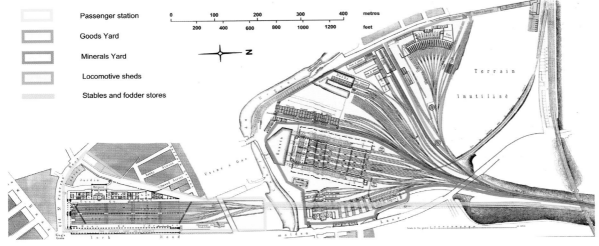

Passenger station

Goods Yard

Minerals Yard

Locomotive sheds

Stables and fodder stores

**2.10**: Great Northern Railway London Terminus, an extract from 1858 plan and sections. (Lacroix, 1866, e-rara)

THE LONDON STATION OF THE GREAT NORTHERN RAILWAY

# THE LONDON STATION – SIGNALLING ARRANGEMENTS

The earliest plan of the London terminus of the GNR is a sketch map of October 1852 by Captain Galton of the Royal Engineers (2.9), who was responsible for inspecting the signalling arrangements on behalf of the Board of Trade.

The accompanying text describes the signalling procedures adopted. Points A to E were located as follows:

A    North end of Copenhagen Tunnel
B    South end of Copenhagen Tunnel
C    West side of goods line embankment, just south of NLR
D    South end of Gasworks Tunnel
E    West side of passenger line embankment, south of junction with goods line

A man at 'A' North of Tunnel to work the Bell Signal to indicate to the Man at 'B' which train is arriving. The Man at 'B' to have a wire to ring to the man at 'C' that a Goods or Coal train is arriving or to the man at 'D' by means of Electric Telegraph that a Passenger train is arriving. The Man at 'C' or 'D' will repeat the signal to 'B' and if all is clear the train will be allowed to come on by the man at 'B' signalling to 'A' to that effect. One of the Semaphores at 'C' to be removed leaving only the two – one for Goods and one for Coals. A double signal to be put up at Junction 'B' for the Goods Station or the new Passenger Station. A Man will be stationed at 'D' who when he gets the Telegraphic Signal from 'B' will repeat it to a post at 'E' which can be seen from 'B'. The double signal at 'B' will regulate the departure as only one signal must show at any one time as 'all right' and the man at 'B' must also have the means of signalling by Electric Telegraph to the man at 'D' that the line is clear or not for the Passenger trains to start.

The engraving of Copenhagen Tunnel and the North London Railway, published in November 1851 (see 9.2, page 108), shows the signal box 'C' but either predates 'B' or leaves it hidden behind a support pillar.

# THE LONDON STATION – GENERAL PLAN

The earliest surviving scaled plan of the London Station was drawn in 1858 by a French team as part of a comprehensive work on railway engineering that was edited by Eugène Lacroix and published in 1866; this is shown in 2.10.

The London Station has been divided into sectors that are treated more fully in subsequent chapters:

Passenger Station in Chapter 3, GNR Passenger Station
Goods Yard in Chapter 4, GNR Goods Station
Locomotive Sheds in Chapter 5, Locomotive Sheds
Stables and fodder stores in Chapter 6, Horse Power
Minerals Yard in Chapter 7, Coal Supply

## ENGAGEMENT WITH MIDLAND RAILWAY AND NORTH LONDON RAILWAY

The GN Railway Lands were bordered by and crossed the railways of several major competitors. The NLR was closely associated with both the LNWR and the Midland Railway (MR), and the latter was keen to extend its services into London. While these companies were strong competitors of the GNR, they also needed to cooperate as they became established. The truly cut-throat competition that had prevailed during George Hudson's reign as railway king ended in 1849 and was replaced with commercial rivalry combined with some grudging cooperation.

Despite authority given under its Act, the NLR was reluctant to construct a junction with the GNR near King's Cross, no doubt influenced by the LNWR. For the GNR such a junction would provide essential rail access to the docks, and it took the matter to Chancery, which ruled in its favour. In June 1853, Joseph Cubitt reported that the work was completed – this line, which connected the Train Assembly Shed and the NLR, can be seen on plan 2.10.

Under an agreement in 1857, full running powers from Hitchin and the use of King's Cross terminus for seven years were granted by the GNR to the MR, primarily to deter the Midland from seeking a line of its own into London (Johns, 1952). The GNR was also to build an engine shed for MR locomotives.

The MR leased the former carriage shed next to the Granary, which was adapted for use as a goods shed. A short office range was added at the south end to handle the paperwork arising from MR goods transhipment. The conversion was completed in July 1858. A stables range was built for the MR in the north-western corner of the goods yard (6.7, page 79).

From 1 February 1858, the MR started the through-running of passenger trains to King's Cross under the powers granted by the GNR in 1857. General goods traffic to London was also started by the MR over the Leicester–Hitchin line, worked from Hitchin by GNR locomotives.

The Midland Roundhouse locomotive shed was completed in February 1859 by the GNR at a cost of some £10,500 and leased to the MR at 6 per cent per annum.

In August 1861 John Jay, the contractor, was instructed to proceed with the North London Incline, the branch which provided double track access to the NLR from the GNR main line at Goods and Mineral Junction, south of Copenhagen Tunnel, via a junction with the line from the goods yard to the NLR. When this opened in July 1862 it facilitated the goods and mineral traffic movements of all three companies.

Meanwhile, in 1858, clearance of part of Agar Town had been authorised for the erection of the Midland Railway's Coal Depot. In 1861 the MR decided to locate their Goods and Mineral Station at Agar Grove. On 5 July 1862 the MR were instructed by the GNR to move all their coal wagons from the goods yard. They also vacated the Midland goods shed for their newly completed Agar Town depot.

The volume of Midland passenger train traffic for the 1862 International Exhibition caused further friction with the GNR, which exhorted the MR to use its own recently completed yard at Agar Town rather than the main passenger station at King's Cross.

In February 1863 the Midland gave notice to terminate the seven years' Traffic Agreement with the GNR, and MR coal traffic to King's Cross goods yard ceased soon thereafter. On 2 January 1865 the MR opened its St Pancras goods depot, an enlargement of the Agar Town depot.

**2.11**: King's Cross Railway Lands in 1871. (OS London Large Scale series)

**2.12**: King's Cross Railway Lands in 1893. (OS, edition 1894–96)

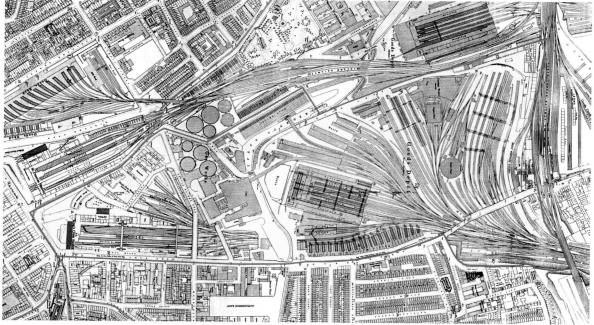

THE KING'S CROSS STORY: 200 YEARS OF HISTORY IN THE RAILWAY LANDS

# MANAGEMENT OF OPERATIONS

Operations of the Company can be divided into direction and management. A Board of Directors was responsible for direction under the guidance of the Chairman. No decision of financial significance could be taken without the sanction of the Board, whose main responsibility was to the shareholders.

The Board appointed the General Manager as the chief administrator who organised day-to-day management of the main departments. These departments and their heads (up to Grouping) were:

Engineering Department – Engineer
Goods Department – Goods Manager
Traffic Department – Superintendent of the Line
Locomotive Department – Locomotive Engineer

The Board of Directors generally met on a Friday throughout the GNR period until 1922, as did also the Executive Committee. Direction was carried out through a hierarchy of committees on which directors sat, and the weekly meetings of the major committees were scheduled to allow decisions to move upwards during the week to the Board meetings on Fridays. At the top of the tree for any major financial decisions was the GNR Executive Committee. The next tier included the Way and Works Committee, which

**2.13**: King's Cross Railway Lands in the urban landscape. (OS, edition 1913–14)

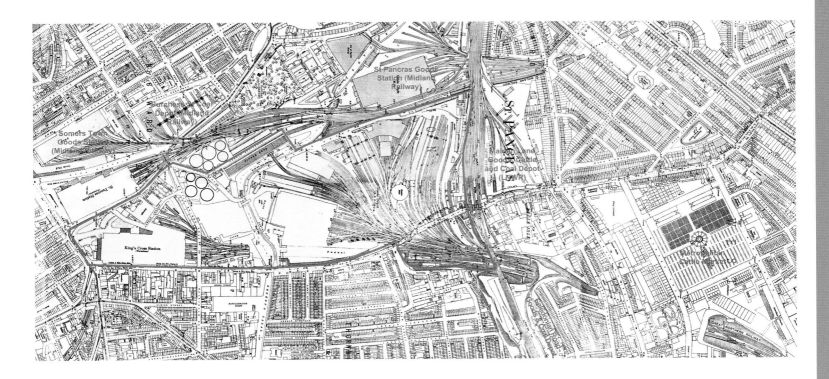

directed the Engineering Department; the Traffic Committee, which directed the Traffic Department; and the Locomotive Committee, which directed the Locomotive Department. Other standing committees relevant to King's Cross included the Hotels Committee and later the Horse Committee. Many ad hoc committees were formed to direct phases of new works or issues that required the directors' attention, such as coordination with the Metropolitan Railway when it developed its underground lines.

Typically, a proposal for new works, such as a new stable, would pass from a Horse Department manager to the Chief Engineer and General Manager, and would be presented by one or more of these officials at the Horse Committee meeting from where the resolution if approved would, depending on the financial implications, seek sanction from the next tiers: the Way and Works Committee and the Board of Directors.

## EVOLUTION OF GNR LONDON STATION

The original layout was simple, with the passenger station and terminus hotel south of the Regent's Canal and the goods and minerals yards and locomotive sheds north of the canal. This concept was essentially preserved over time.

By 1871 (2.11, page 34) the northern areas of the goods yard were filling with sidings as part of the Coal Depot. The Western Coal Drops were constructed in 1860 alongside the Coal and Stone Basin, with a timber viaduct alongside the basin. Timber viaducts were also constructed across the canal both to the coal drops in Cambridge Street (1866) and to the Imperial Gas Light and Coke Company (1867).

South of the canal, the Imperial Gas Company in 1860 bought the leases of housing in Agar Town and erected two groups of telescopic gasholders there.

By 1894 (2.12) the housing terraces south of the canal had been replaced by the expanding Suburban Station, although some new housing was created in the form of the Stanley and Culross Buildings.

There were now three gasworks tunnels, the original one being flanked on the west by a tunnel opened in 1878 and on the east by one opened 1892. There had also been an increase in the sidings in the northern part of the yard.

The last decade of the nineteenth century saw substantial warehouse and office expansion:

- 1888: Roofs added between Midland Goods Shed and Eastern Transit Shed and between Midland Goods Shed and old passenger shed.
- 1896–97: Roof added over the Potato Market roadway serving the thirty-nine warehouses.
- 1897: Wharf Road extended in goods yard expansion. Coal and Fish Offices extended with arches below road used for stables.
- 1897–99: Western Goods Shed built, a two-level warehouse for outward goods (tracks entering on both floors) over the infilled Coal and Stone Basin.
- 1897–99: Western Coal Drops converted to goods shed, also for outward goods, and offices built on second floor. Plimsoll Viaduct rebuilt in iron on brick arches.

It was only in the early twentieth century that additional land became available on the gasworks site south of the canal to accommodate additional railway facilities. Gas manufacture ceased in February 1904, and the GNR acquired part of the land from the gasworks in 1911.

## LONDON STATION IN THE URBAN LANDSCAPE

To the west, the Midland Railway built St Pancras Goods Station (2.13, page 35) in King's Road, which opened in January 1865, an enlargement of the 1862 Agar Town goods station. Both phases required major clearance of residential properties, justified on the grounds that these were slums of the worst kind. The Midland's Purchese Street Coal Depot, completed later the same year, involved further clearance of Somers Town.

In 1866 the Midland Railway obtained parliamentary consent to demolish the remaining houses in Agar Town and build the railway line into St Pancras Station over the land. The station opened in 1868. The Midland Railway's application to build Somers Town Goods Depot in 1874, on the site where the British Library now stands, resulted in the demolition of 4,000 homes that housed 10,000 people.

By 1866 St Pancras had become the most densely populated part of the London metropolis. Railway clearances must bear much of the responsibility for this; forcing evicted communities into ever more tightly packed accommodation.

By the third quarter of the nineteenth century, the Railway Lands were set in a highly urban and industrialised landscape. North of the Railway Lands, and west of Copenhagen Tunnel, lay the Metropolitan Cattle Market with its surrounding pens, slaughterhouses, and public houses. This exerted a strong influence on the neighbouring small-scale industry, much of which had direct connections with the cattle market. Belle Isle, to the south of the market, continued to be the site of numerous noxious enterprises.

The NLR constrained further northwards expansion of the Railway Lands. Here the LNWR, another competitor, built a goods, cattle and coal depot.

While some of the gasholders lie just outside the perimeter of the King's Cross railway lands, they are treated as lying inside. Their visual impact was a vital feature, recognised by moving gasholder frames into the King's Cross Central redevelopment (page 197).

# three

# GNR Passenger Station

## MAIN PASSENGER STATION

**3.1**: Arrival of Queen Victoria at King's Cross Station, 1853. (SSPL/NRM)

The strength and simplicity of Lewis Cubitt's design for the main passenger station is seen in 3.1. It was constructed of yellow stock brick. Two lunette windows reveal the ribs of the arrival and departure shed roofs behind, separated by the central projecting clock tower and projecting sections at the margins. An arched arcade at the front provided a concourse, while the eastern side featured an arched opening to a cab road. The Great Northern Hotel is seen on the left beyond the western offices.

# PLAN AND SECTION

The earliest surviving plan of the Main Passenger Station is shown below in 3.2.

The legend that accompanies the plan has been translated as follows:

LEGEND

| | | | |
|---|---|---|---|
| 1–4 | Registration offices | 21 | Ladies toilets |
| 5–6 | Telegraph offices | 22 | Men's WC |
| 7–8 | Resident Engineer's office | 23 | Refreshments |
| 9 | Men's WC | 24–25 | Traction Maintenance Engineer's offices |
| 10 | Second Class ladies waiting room | 26–29 | Superintendent's offices |
| 11 | Second Class waiting room | 30 | Men's WC |
| 12 | Ladies toilets | 31 | Lost luggage |
| 13 | Booking hall | 32–33 | Carmen |
| 14 | Ticket office | 34 | Down parcels office |
| 15 | Stationmaster | 35 | Parcels yard |
| 16 | Safe room | 36–38 | Police |
| 17 | Station Inspector | 39–41 | Guards |
| 18 | Books and papers stall | 42 | Yard |
| 19 | First Class ladies waiting room | 43 | Men's WC |
| 20 | First Class waiting room | | |

**3.2**: Plan of Main Passenger Station, extract from 1858 plan and sections. (Lacroix, 1866, e-rara)

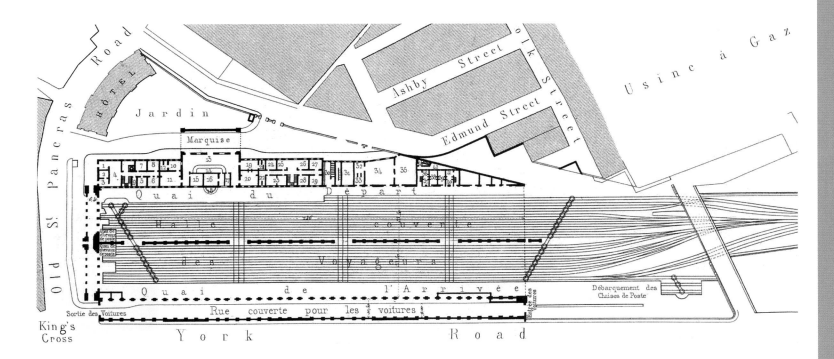

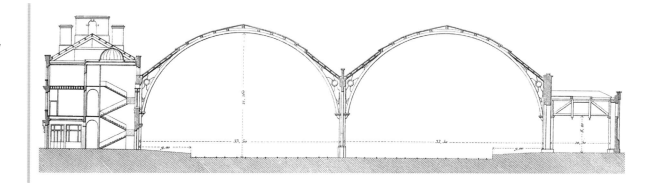

**3.3**: Cross-section of the station, extract from 1858 plan and sections. (Lacroix, 1866, e-rara)

The cross-sectional elevation from the same source (3.3) is drawn from a west–east line that runs through one of the two staircases of the Western Range, the three-storey offices aligned alongside the departure platform, presumably that opposite the engineers' and superintendent's offices, as the *porte cochère* or *'marquise'* is not seen. The Western Range housed the facilities listed in the legend.

At the south end were the Registration Offices (Nos 1–4) into which Leopold Redpath, the King's Cross fraudster (Hayes, 2013) moved in 1852 from the Company's temporary headquarters in Maiden Lane. Promoted to Registrar in 1854, he would, over eight years from 1848, forge share certificates and sell counterfeit shares to a value of £253,000, worth over £20 million today, enjoying a lavish and cultured lifestyle until discovered and deported to Australia.

## ARRIVAL AND DEPARTURE SHEDS AND CAB ROAD

The semi-circular arches spanning the Arrival and Departure Sheds were each 71ft (22m) high and 105ft (32m) wide (3.4). The timber ribs supporting the arches sprang from iron stanchions mounted on the two outer walls and on a third wall that ran down the middle of the station, pierced by broad elliptical arches. The ribs were 20ft (6m) apart. The plan (3.2) shows forty-one ribs running the length of the sheds, providing a shed length of 800ft (244m). Each rib was laminated, being made up of sixteen 1½in (38mm) boards screwed and bolted together.

The upper five-eighths of the roof were glazed, the remaining lower part being slated over timber boards (3.4). The thrust of the arched roof was taken on the west side by the three-storey office block (3.3). On the east side the thrust was taken by wooden flying buttresses spanning the cab road.

The single arrival platform was on the right of the Arrivals Shed. From here it was but a few steps to the cab rank. This was paved with wooden blocks laid on a sub-stratum of concrete, the station thereby being spared some of the din of vehicles and horses. Both arrival and departure platforms were paved with York stone.

The single departure platform was similarly located in the Departure Shed. Departing passengers would arrive via Station Road, a cab road leading off Old St Pancras Road to the station, where they would disembark under the *porte cochère* (canopy) over the entrance to the booking office ('*marquise*' in 3.2) and make their way through the Booking Hall to the Ticket Office. Here they would 'book' a ticket and make their way to the departure platform with the help of porters if required (3.5). They could await their train in the Refreshment Room (3.5), managed by the lessee of the Great Northern Hotel, Joseph Dethier.

A second arrival platform was built in 1862 to prevent delays in discharging trains, but until 1893 there was only one main line departure platform that was used by forty trains per day. Two more platforms were added that year, one on either side of the central wall. That same year, two-storey offices were built over the cab road together with an iron footbridge to link the offices on the west and east sides.

The eastern (arrivals) train shed roof timbers had deteriorated over time and in 1866–67 the wooden ribs were replaced by iron ribs in the same configuration. A travelling timber stage, as had been used for the larger shed at St Pancras, was used for the work, being placed in storage on completion in anticipation of further use for the western train shed roof. This was replaced twenty years later, over 1886–87.

**3.5**: Christmas Eve, 1852, in the Departure Shed at the newly opened station, John Gordon Thomson. (Courtesy of the Ironbridge Gorge Museum Trust – the Sir Arthur Elton Collection)

**3.6**: Clock tower with St Pancras clock in background. (Matt Brown, *Londonist*)

## TIMEKEEPING

For many years, railway time was the only standard time in the British Isles. London time was derived from the Royal Observatory at Greenwich, with chronometers set to the master time and transported around the rail network. From the 1850s, time signals from Greenwich could be sent around the rail network via electric telegraph. While standard time was increasingly taken up around the country, it was not till the Time Act of 1880 that Greenwich time became legally binding.

The station clock tower was a feature that signalled the importance of railway time, complemented by clocks within stations, typically on the departure platforms. In 3.6 opposite we see the lordly clock tower of St Pancras keeping an eye on its humbler neighbour.

The clock tower that separates the lunette windows of the Arrival and Departures sheds at King's Cross is 120ft (37m) high. It was fitted internally with rooms and staircases leading to the clock room and other compartments. The grand feature of the tower is the clock itself, the four faces of which are composed of slate. The clock was manufactured by Dent, three of its clock faces remain today, while three bells (bass, tenor and treble) were obtained from John Murphy, an Irish foundry. The largest, weighing 29cwt (1,475kg), was for striking the hour; its sonorous peal had been frequently heard at the Great Exhibition, where it had received a medal. The two other bells struck the quarters for a few years.

The firm of E. Dent & Co. was commissioned in 1965 to replace the old clock mechanism with a simpler electric one. It ceased to trade the following year.

## GREAT NORTHERN HOTEL

The Great Northern Hotel (3.7) was designed by Lewis Cubitt, its curved shape in plan following the curved approach of Old St Pancras Road to the New Road. The building forms three sections separated by two staircase bays that present a distinct decorative feature. The curve of the building is entirely taken up by the central section, the two outer sections being straight.

The curve allowed the hotel and its 100 guest bedrooms to turn their back on the tenements of Somers Town, and instead face the station across a large garden. The curve also served the internal aesthetics, avoiding long featureless bedroom corridors.

Built over 1852–54 out of the same yellow stock brick as the station, the building was of fireproof construction, with thick walls separating rooms. It had a basement, ground floor and five further floors, including the roof space.

Joseph Dethier, a hotelier of No. 210 Piccadilly, had written to the GNR in November 1850 proposing to erect and rent a hotel on the company's property at King's Cross. He was closely involved in the design of the hotel and accepted as the tenant of both the hotel and the Refreshment Rooms on the main station departure platform (3.5) for a period of twenty-two years from 1 July 1853.

In 1873 Dethier's trustees requested an extension of the lease, but the Company declined and decided to manage the hotel itself from 1875.

## CONNECTIONS WITH METROPOLITAN RAILWAY

Work began on the Metropolitan Railway, the world's first underground railway, in 1859. Completion was delayed by a burst in the underground sewer carrying the Fleet River, but the line opened from Paddington (Bishops Road) to Farringdon on 10 January 1863.

King's Cross Metropolitan Station was sited at the junction of Gray's Inn Road and Pentonville Road. The painting of the station (3.8, page 46) shows two lines of mixed-gauge track designed to take both standard (GNR) and broad-gauge (GWR) trains, with the common line nearest the platform; both trains shown are broad gauge. The gaslights, iron ribs and footbridge, as well as the passengers, contribute to a studied image of space and elegance not generally associated with underground railway stations. Illustrations from the time generally depict middle-class passengers using the underground, despite the high number of workmen's fares and third-class tickets sold by the Metropolitan Railway.

To connect with the Metropolitan Railway, the GNR built a single track 'up' line along York Road (formerly Maiden Lane) and a 'down' line that followed a curved alignment on the west side of the station, passing under the Great Northern Hotel, a section of track that became known as the Hotel Curve. A GNR service to Farringdon Street started on 1 October 1863.

Soon afterwards, in 1866, the track was widened between King's Cross and Farringdon, and a four-track railway opened to Moorgate Street. The additional tracks were owned by the Metropolitan Railway but were used mainly by other railway companies. They were known as the 'Widened Lines'.

**3.8**: Junction of the Midland, Great Northern and Metropolitan Railways at King's Cross, 1868. (Mary Evans)

A train on the GNR–Metropolitan up line is seen approaching from the right in 3.8 onto the recently constructed Midland lines that provided a service to Moorgate Street before the St Pancras terminus had opened. A steam locomotive, heading a train bound for Paddington, has stopped at the Metropolitan Railway platform on the left. The Metropolitan initially ordered eighteen tank locomotives, a key feature of which was condensing equipment to reduce the amount of steam escaping while trains were in tunnels.

## YORK ROAD STATION

Initially Farringdon trains had to reverse out of the main station on their way south, but in July 1865 a platform at York Road (3.10) was approved and this opened on 1 January 1866. The first scheduled service was to the London Chatham & Dover Railway (LC&D) in March 1866. At the same time a footbridge was built from the north end of Platform 1 of the main station to the new station at York Road, for the benefit of passengers alighting from up Moorgate trains.

## SUBURBAN STATION

York Road Station was not followed by a corresponding platform on the west side until 1873; this was located where the Hotel Curve emerged from the tunnel (3.11), and was known as King's Cross (Suburban).

In 1873 two platforms were provided for local trains, built outside the main station on the west side, and became King's Cross (Local). The locomotive shed immediately to the west was demolished in 1874, and a new locomotive depot with three roads built in 1875 so that suburban platforms could be provided on the site of the first locomotive shed. These were enclosed by a long brick wall that supported the roof of the new platforms (3.11). A new locomotive turntable was constructed nearby.

A third platform was added in 1875 together with a fourth beyond the Hotel Curve platform.

The need for extra space was a constant operations issue during the first half-century. In 1889, drastic plans were drawn up to expand the station to the west by purchasing Eley's Cartridge Case Works on Cheney Street and removing the GN Hotel and the Parcel Stables. A booking hall was to be built to the south, giving ready access to platforms as an end-on station. A less drastic option was adopted – moving the Engine Shed to the west and adapting the Suburban Station.

By 1892 the Engine Shed was no longer required as part of the locomotive depot, giving space in King's Cross (Local) for three tracks, with two good platforms and a booking office in Cheney Street. Over the following three years the roof and platforms at the Local Station were altered and the enlarged station was opened for passengers in April 1895.

In 1893 two sets of sidings were created for milk and for horse and carriage traffic between the Suburban Station and Battle Bridge Road. The sidings included a Horse Loading Wharf and a dock for loading carriages, with two sidings separated by a triangular platform. A larger triangular platform, also served by two sidings, dealt with the fast-growing milk traffic.

## FRONT OF MAIN STATION

The curve of Old St Pancras Road left isolated a triangle of land up to the New Road, opposite the station entrance, which the Company purchased at the first opportunity in 1851. From this moment, a large amount of the Board's time was spent in considering how the land could best be used.

One of the first tasks would be to realign Old St Pancras Road. This occurred in the late 1860s when the Midland Railway rearranged the whole area as part of its London terminus at St Pancras. The triangle was now within the station precinct. Houses on this land were in the company's possession by June 1871 and were being cleared as rapidly as possible.

In 1873, Sir George Gilbert Scott offered his services in the preparation of plans, both for the station frontage and the utilisation of spare ground in front of the station, but the Company was not ready to use his services.

Plans were drawn up for a covered way at the front of the station serving cabs and passengers, but were deferred. Early photographs (3.12) show the arcade that formed the lower part of the façade, a lightweight structure with a glazed roof supported on cast-iron columns. By the mid-1880s, the Post Office Authorities had leased a site at the front of the station for a building to accommodate their parcels business and schemes were being drawn up for erecting shops and offices for several large customers of the Company on the remainder of the land without interfering with the Parcels Post Office.

In the event, the Post Office gave up their premises in 1888 after five years, which stimulated further plans for offices of two and three storeys, partly to meet the demands for extra

**3.12**: The front of King's Cross Station, 1903. (CLSAC)

accommodation of several of the company's departments. These went out to tender and a contract was awarded in November 1888 for £22,000. The works stalled when the Engineer of the Metropolitan Railway Company raised a serious question over the Metropolitan Railway Tunnel. His Consulting Engineer had advised that the only way the safety of the tunnel could be secured was by building an inverted arch under that part of the tunnel upon which the buildings were to be erected.

The Engineer of the GNR reported that, owing to the heavy traffic on both the Midland and GN lines, it would be very difficult to carry out the work in a safe and satisfactory manner. He asked that the question of erecting buildings on this site be reconsidered. In June 1890, a scheme was prepared for a building of five storeys on the Euston Road, and an additional building in the GN Hotel garden that would include a Shareholders' Meeting Room and thirty rooms for offices.

None of these schemes were implemented. Instead the 'native village', as it became known, was allowed to grow organically, particularly after the First World War, providing the offices and shops that had been planned but not realised over previous decades. The arcade that formed the lower part of the façade was increasingly masked by a clutter of small buildings, huts and shelters, which were finally swept away in the 1960s when the Victoria Line was constructed. In the 1970s the arcade at the front was replaced by a covered concourse with a green-edged canopy.

## IMPERIAL GAS COMPANY

The St Pancras works of the Imperial Gas Light and Coke Company, which manufactured town gas from coal, were described in Chapter 1. Both demand for and production of gas varied through the day, requiring storage on site to absorb these fluctuations. This took the form of substantial telescopic gasholders. Early versions were replaced in the 1860s, and reconstructed and enlarged in the 1880s. The most decorative were Gasholder 8 and Gasholders 10, 11 and 12, three gasholders with linked frames that were known as the 'Siamese Triplet', a design unique in Great Britain and with deeper gasholders than any previously constructed.

The St Pancras works of the Imperial Gas Light and Coke Company ceased to manufacture gas from February 1904, and the word spread that the company was intent on giving up its King's Cross site altogether. This triggered a series of meetings in 1905–06 between the Midland and GN companies in which they recognised that each had an interest and agreed that neither should act without consulting the other, nor enter negotiation without prior communication with the other party. The areas on the ground in which each party had an exclusive interest were agreed, with the remaining area being open for negotiation.

The GN Company could see important savings in maintenance costs and operational efficiencies by the demolition of Congreve Street Bridge, Battle Bridge and the timber viaduct serving the gasworks. These features can be seen in 2.12 on page 34.

The GNR acquired about 5½ acres (2.2ha) of land from the gasworks in 1911, and Congreve Street was removed. The retort houses, purifiers, boiler house, barge dock and warehouse were taken down to ground level in 1912.

As will be seen from many images, the gasholders, more than almost any other structures, evoked the spirit of the Railway Lands. They survived the closure of the gasworks and the transition to natural gas, but all bar Gasholder 8 and the Siamese Triplet were demolished in 2001 ahead of the construction of the Channel Tunnel Rail Link. The four listed gasholders were dismantled so that their frames and lattice girders could be re-erected as part of King's Cross Central.

## GERMAN GYMNASIUM

*Die Turnhalle*, as it was first known, was designed by Edward Gruning and built for the German Gymnastic Society in Old St Pancras Road. Opened in 1865, it was the first purpose-built public gymnasium in the country (3.13), and the first to hold exercise classes for women. Within a decade half its members were English.

Ernest Ravenstein, one of the directors of the German Gymnastics Society, was responsible for organising the National Olympian Games in London in 1866, a regional precursor to the Games we see

3.13: German Gymnasium with ropes hanging from the timber roof support ribs. (CLSAC)

today. The indoor events at the Games were held at the new German Gymnasium, while the outdoor events were held on the River Thames and at Crystal Palace. The Games were a major success, attracting over 10,000 spectators, and indoor events continued annually until the White City Olympic Games were held in 1908.

The German Gymnasium was leased by the GNR in 1908. It was purchased by the GNR in July 1916 and converted into offices. It suffered damage in an air raid in July 1917.

## HORSE OMNIBUS

The horse omnibus became an increasingly popular means of transport between London's termini, and the GNR found itself trying to meet this demand. In 1882 the General Manager, Henry Oakley, advised the Board that:

> These vehicles have become so popular, and are in such demand that we have been obliged to refuse a very large number indeed of intending passengers by our line. We have now 10 omnibuses, and all of them are in active service. We further find that for families and large establishments, a two-horse omnibus is sometimes asked for, and as we have no two-horse omnibuses we are obliged to send two of our small ones. I would therefore ask your authority to build 6 more one-horse omnibuses, and 2 two-horse omnibuses.

## COMPETITION FOR PASSENGER TRAFFIC

Passenger journeys by rail in London increased from about 174 million in 1875 to 400 million in 1896. However, the share of rail in passenger traffic fell from 60 per cent to 40 per cent over the same period (Simmons 1986), as its dominance was undermined by the development of cheaper modes of transport: first bus services and then, from 1870, trams, both horse-drawn. The competition not only captured much of rail's market share but so reduced fares that certain rail services became unprofitable, notably workers' trains.

To quote Simmons, 'In late Victorian London the horse took his revenge on the locomotive.'

# GNR Goods Station

# four

## THE GOODS BUSINESS

The goods business, or the reception and onward delivery of the inward traffic and the loading and dispatch of the outward traffic, took place out of public gaze in its own private world, one that operated twenty-four hours a day.

This chapter is largely devoted to the infrastructure that was provided to support goods and mineral traffic. Mineral traffic divides into coal traffic and stone and brick; Chapter 7 addresses the coal traffic and Chapter 8 the goods and other mineral traffic, including stone and brick, but the lines between these chapters and the present chapter are not sharply drawn.

The receipts for passenger and goods traffic at the King's Cross terminus are not directly comparable, due to lack of data, but may be related to national trends for the last fifty years of Victoria's reign.

In 1845, before the GNR was established, passenger receipts were twice goods traffic receipts. By 1852, when the GNR was operational, the value of goods traffic was almost that of passenger traffic and five years later had overtaken passenger traffic in value. Between 1860 and the end of the century, goods receipts increased by around 350 per cent, whereas passenger receipts increased by only 40 per cent (Wade, 1900). We have seen in the last chapter how, in revenue terms, growth in passenger traffic was largely offset by pressure on fares from competition with bus and tram services.

| Year | Weight moved (million tons) | Goods traffic (£M) | Unit cost (£/ton) | Passenger traffic (£M) | Growth of goods revenue (% p.a.) | Growth of passenger revenue (% p.a.) |
|------|------|------|------|------|------|------|
| 1845 |     | 2.74  |      | 5.48  |    |   |
| 1850 |     | 6.38  |      | 7.50  | 18 | 6 |
| 1860 | 90  | 14.68 | 0.16 | 13.18 | 9  | 6 |
| 1870 | 150 | 24.12 | 0.16 |       | 5  |   |
| 1880 | 235 | 35.76 | 0.15 |       | 4  |   |
| 1890 | 303 | 42.22 | 0.14 |       | 2  |   |
| 1898 | 379 | 49.22 | 0.13 | 18.13 | 2  | 1 |

However limited the data, the strong growth of the goods business from the 1850s to the 1870s and the increasing importance of goods traffic to the GNR in the second half of the nineteenth century appear undeniable. It may be assumed that growth at King's Cross was somewhat below national averages, as the GN started decentralising its goods handling operations from the 1860s onwards. By the 1880s King's Cross was the principal goods yard among many GN yards in the metropolis.

Coal traffic moved at the dictates of collieries, coal merchants and industrial users, and the GN was determined to capture a large part of this trade from seaborne carriers.

Merchandise traffic may be divided into agricultural produce and general goods. The east coast of Britain supplied much of the grain, potatoes, fish and cattle to an ever-growing metropolis, and the GN was well positioned to serve the rich farming areas of East Anglia, Lincolnshire, Yorkshire and beyond. The railway allowed perishable fruit and vegetables to be sourced for the metropolis from much further afield than the market gardens that had surrounded London.

## LAYOUT OF GOODS STATION

Within its physical constraints, the layout of the goods station adapted continuously to the nature and volume of goods traded and to the influence of the competition, particularly over the first fifty years. Traders were not slow to draw comparisons with the support they would receive from competing railway companies, if this worked to their advantage.

Two snapshots are presented of the goods yard layout at the start (4.1) and end (8.2, page 95) of this period. For a more detailed picture, the reader is referred to Haslam (2016).

The 1858 plan shows the goods yard little-changed from its beginnings, with the Temporary Passenger Station converted into the Potato Market, for which an additional warehouse had been built along York Road (formerly Maiden Lane). A warehouse devoted to traffic in lime was sited nearby.

While the general level around the main goods sheds shown in 4.1 was at 24.2m (79ft) OD, the Coal Depot had a courtyard some 3m lower at 21.2m (70ft) OD, close to original ground level, in order to accommodate the Eastern Coal Drops. The rail tracks on the eastern approaches to the drops were at 26.7m OD. On the south-west side of the depot, an inclined roadway, a feature obvious today, provided cart access to the lower level. On the north side, the brick and stone yard was at around 26.0m OD, as was much of the rest of the yard. Along the canal, the retaining wall provided the opportunity to construct stables below the higher-level road, which became known as Wharf Road.

The construction of the Midland Railway's Agar Grove goods yard caused Seymour Clarke, General Manager, to observe in 1864:

> The whole question of accommodation at King's Cross is a very large and difficult one … as, compared with the Midland Company's new yard, we are at a disadvantage, their premises lying to the front, while ours are some distance up Maiden Lane, and the access to them is up a somewhat steep Bridge over the Canal.

Congestion at King's Cross goods yard was partially resolved in 1865 by providing additional accommodation for wagons at Holloway Road.

Seymour Clarke's successor, Henry Oakley, also grappled with the layout, noting in 1888:

We have now a large area of land used for stacking Coal, it was envisaged to keep this for Coal purposes so long as we could spare the room, but it has now become essential, especially for the busy traffic of the winter, to occupy the present stacking ground with sidings. The scheme proposed will provide for 472 additional wagons, 280 of which could be reached by carts. The provision of this accommodation will enable us to defer for a time the further consideration of the removal of the Locomotive Department, and which being so costly it is desirable not to entertain until we are obliged to face it.

Another persistent source of concern was the churning of the surfaces of the yard, caused by horse shunting. Although all the goods station area was eventually paved with granite, paving proceeded very slowly.

## GOODS TRANSHIPMENT

The railway goods shed allowed the transfer of goods under cover between road and rail on one level. The idea of interconnecting road, rail and canal traffic in one building had been initiated by Pickford at Camden Goods Station in 1841 (Darley, 2013). Combined with warehousing, it allowed goods services to be extended to a wide range of customers.

At King's Cross, canal boats had access into the Granary Basin (4.2), and thus into the two transit sheds, where all three forms of transport can be seen, with transfer from one form to another across a 'bank' being facilitated by a battalion of cranes (4.3). The water level in the canal was at about 21.0m OD, with the bank at approx. 25.5m OD. The cranes were therefore essential for transferring between the bank and a barge below.

Warehousing of general incoming and outgoing goods proved more controversial and was swiftly abandoned by the Company, although later taken up in some tenanted premises.

A 10-ton crane on the north-west side of the Granary Basin was used to transfer heavy goods from rail to canal. Barges could also access the Coal and Stone Basin immediately downstream of St Pancras Locks, where they could be loaded from the rail side with coal, stone and bricks.

However, canal movements declined towards the end of the nineteenth century and first the Coal and Stone Basin was filled in about 1898 for construction of the Western Goods Shed, followed by the Granary Basin in about 1920.

## ENTRANCE FROM YORK ROAD

One of the two entrances to the GNR's goods yard is shown in 4.4, a view from the east side of York Road (York Way since 1938). The Regent's Canal widened at this point for coal barges to moor alongside the Imperial Gas Company's works on the left, of which the chimney of one of the retorts is prominent.

**4.1**: A plan showing the layout of GNR's goods yard, extract from 1858 plan and sections, overlaid by author. (Lacroix, 1866, e-rara)

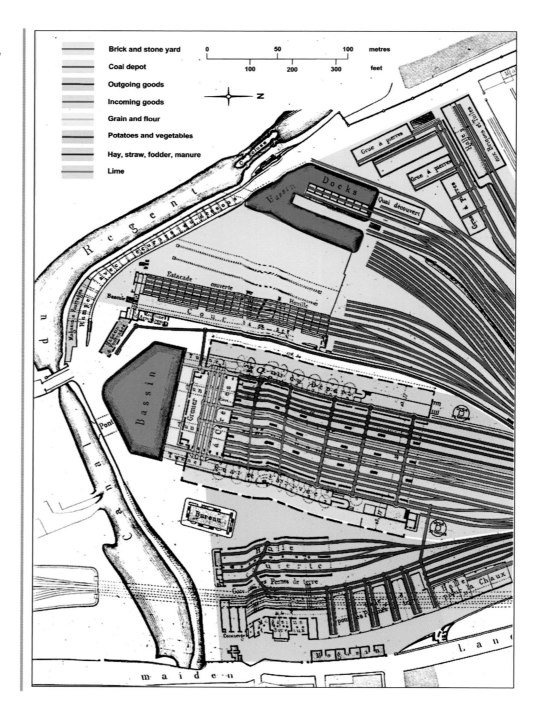

THE KING'S CROSS STORY: 200 YEARS OF HISTORY IN THE RAILWAY LANDS

The gateway led to a private road. This ran parallel to the canal up to the Coal Depot, which lay beyond the chimney of the hydraulic power station, seen in the middle distance. Road-borne deliveries either left the goods yard via this gateway or crossed the canal at Somers Bridge, seen more clearly in the close-up in 4.5, on their way to Cheney Road, Edmund Street and thence the main road network on the west side of the goods yard.

Fronting the road from the right of 4.4, we can identify the gate lodge, the East Handyside Canopy that led to the Potato Market, Potato Market Warehouse 39, the Midland Goods Shed offices and the GN goods office (now Regeneration House). The Eastern Transit Shed south façade appears on the left of these offices and the Granary warehouse rises above them. 'Kilner Bros Ltd' is seen on the ribbed roof of the Midland Goods Shed, the southern part of which they leased as a bottle warehouse.

The close-up in 4.5 reveals more clearly the high-level viaduct supplying coal to the gasworks. Below this, the ridged profile of the six bays of Wiggins' Stables is seen above Somers Bridge. On this side of the bridge the towpath rises to cross the entrance tunnel to Granary Basin, not to be infilled for another twenty years. On the far side of this basin the substantial three-storey building behind the viaduct is the Provender Stables, while hidden behind is the boiler house of the hydraulic station with its chimney at the south end the only part visible.

Above left: **4.2**: Granary Warehouse showing two barges entering the Granary via the central tunnels, and horse-drawn carts lined up against the southern wall to receive sacks of grain via chutes, ILN 28 May 1853. (CRT)

Above right: **4.3**: Western Transit Shed showing the cart road on left, canal access centrally, and rail wagons on the right, with cranes mounted on 'bank', ILN 28 May 1853. (CRT)

## GRANARY, TRANSIT SHEDS AND TRAIN ASSEMBLY SHED

When built in 1850, King's Cross was the world's largest goods station, centred on the Inwards and Outwards Transit Sheds and the iron-roofed marshalling area between them (4.6), which together occupied an area almost 600ft (183m) long by 350ft (107m) wide.

4.4: The York Road entrance to the goods yard c.1900. (David Millbank Challis collection)

4.5: The hub of the goods yard c.1900, with Granary Basin and a concentration of features on all sides. (David Millbank Challis collection)

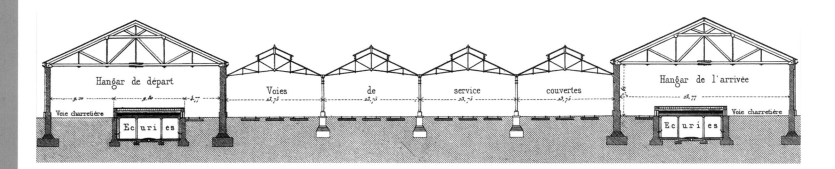

4.6: Sectional elevation through Transit Sheds and Train Assembly Shed, an extract from 1858 plan and sections. (Lacroix, 1866, e-rara)

John Weale (1851) described the complex admirably:

The building is divided into three portions, by means of longitudinal walls, separating respectively on the east and the west a subsidiary shed for either the in or out goods traffic, consisting of two side cart-roads, running longitudinally and parallel to the rails, from which they are separated by a rather wide platform for the reception and classification of the goods; only one line of rails exists in the portion walled off for the particular purpose of the in and out goods trains. A series of turntables on these rails enables the waggons to pass into the centre part of the shed, as soon as they are loaded or unloaded, through a corresponding number of sliding doors, exactly opposite to other doors in the outer walls, communicating with the access roads. The central portion of the shed is divided into 4 bays, with 3 sets of rails in each, to allow of the making up or dividing of 12 trains under cover. The roofs over this portion are of wrought iron; those of the loading and unloading sheds are principally of timber.

In each of the unloading and loading sheds there are 18 cranes for the purpose of assisting the manipulation of the goods. A set of traps in the platform also afford facilities for the barges from the Canal to receive or discharge their goods directly. Similar facilities are offered in the great end warehouse, which also communicates directly with the Canal by means of a tunnel passing under the access road. There is a rather large basin formed for the reception of the barges employed in this part of the traffic, leading by a short cut into the Regent's Canal.

**4.7**: Main Goods Shed, looking south, 1981. (Malcolm Tucker)

The Granary, which fronted the Train Assembly Shed, was completed in 1852. It received grain from the north by rail and, after storage on floors 1–5, moved it on by canal and road.

The Eastern and Western Goods Offices were erected in front of the Inwards and Outwards Sheds respectively in phases over 1860 to the 1870s, to accommodate the ever-increasing numbers of clerical staff required to deal with the paperwork associated with the growing goods business.

Although the main goods shed, the Train Assembly Shed, had been much modified by then, particularly after the introduction of capstan shunting, an impression of the 580ft long structure can be seen in 4.7, looking south and a little east, thereby avoiding the western bay which had experienced the greatest alterations in the form of an additional floor for offices.

## POTATO MARKET, MIDLAND GOODS SHED AND HANDYSIDE CANOPIES

Formerly the great potato market of London was in Tooley Street, Southwark, supplied by coastal shipping to Thames wharves. The GN was the first railway company to establish a large potato depot for London, its location more convenient for supply to Covent Garden. As the market grew, other railway companies entered the trade, and by the 1860s the entire traffic in the carriage of potatoes had been diverted to the railways, the GN foremost among them.

The release of the Temporary Passenger Station from passenger duties in 1852 provided the opportunity to convert it into a potato market. Over the next five years some £20,000 was spent on providing warehouse accommodation for leasing to traders, including a 150ft (46m) by 40ft (12m) warehouse on three floors and some thirty other warehouses to serve around thirty-five traders. The volumes traded grew quickly and, for the potato merchants, exposed a lack of facilities to receive their consignments and inadequate storage, which compelled them to move the potatoes on promptly after

removal from the company's wagons. Lack of sidings led to major blockages, with up to 1,000 wagons waiting to be unloaded.

The complaints of the potato salesmen led to alterations and extensions in 1864 that cost £40,000. The whole of the old passenger terminus was set aside as the area of the new market, on which the Company built thirty-six warehouses fitted with dry and ventilated storage cellars. Sidings were provided for removing potatoes from railway trucks and for loading the drays for delivery to dealers in Covent Garden Market and elsewhere throughout the metropolis.

According to an article and engraving of 1864 (4.8) that purported to show the existing market, the GN's potato trade had been conducted by thirty-five merchants, who carried on their business, before the 1864 improvements, in 'little wooden huts'. In fact, the image shows the temporary site and shacks that briefly accommodated the potato trade while the warehouses were under construction. The huts shown would not have cost £1,000 each and attracted the rental of £40 per year that traders were used to paying. The engraving shows a backdrop of the Midland Railway's Agar Town goods depot on the far side of a palisade fence separating GN from MR land, suggesting that

**4.8**: The Potato Market before the completion of the 1864 warehouses, as seen in the *Illustrated Times*, 1 October 1864. (CLSAC)

the wooden huts were a temporary measure in the north-west corner of the site, to which sidings had by then already been laid. Yet the stables that were a feature of this corner of the goods yard are not shown on the engraving. Artistic licence appears once again to have created a conundrum.

The GN was put on its mettle again by a further complaint from the potato tradesmen in 1888 drawing attention to the need for a vegetable market alongside the Potato Market, and therefore for a light roof to cover certain areas. This was to protect the space between the Potato Market and Midland Goods Shed and the space between the Midland Goods Shed and the main goods shed, both covers to be carried northwards as far as possible.

The traders were in a strong bargaining position, drawing comparison with facilities provided by the Midland Railway, which was actively encouraging changes of allegiance. The GN acceded to covering the whole of the market with a glass roof supported by iron columns at a cost of more than £20,000. Additional potato stores were added at the south end, bringing the total number of warehouses to thirty-nine.

In 1896, the tradesmen once again successfully complained of the lack of cover, this time over the road used for delivery carts that ran between York Road and the potato warehouses.

## COAL DEPOT

When describing the Eastern Coal Drops, John Weale (1851) supplied a clear journalist's account of what was intended:

The works projected, and of which the execution is already so far advanced as to allow an opinion to be formed of the contemplated arrangements, are designed to form 4 large groups of coal-stores, of 50 bays (25 bays or cells on each side of a spine wall), each capable of containing 70 tons, or a grand total of 15,200 [sic] tons. A very ingenious contrivance allows the coal to pass from the waggon to the lower level of the store without serious shock, and obviates the danger of comminuting [i.e. fragmenting] the materials. In the floor of the stores are a series of shoots, six to each bay, through which the coals can either be discharged in bulk, or their flow can be regulated so as to allow of their being easily put in sacks.

These were supplemented by the Western Coal Drops in 1860, and by the Cambridge Street Coal Depot from 1866. Over time, trade moved increasingly to Cambridge Street, and to level sidings in the goods yard where coal was handled manually, largely to avoid the fragmentation and consequent wastage caused by the original drops.

In 1875–76, part of the Eastern Coal Drops was converted into five warehouses to be let to private traders. This policy was applied to the fifteen southern pairs of bays, leaving the ten northern pairs as coal drops. From 1878, some of the Eastern Coal Drops' traffic was diverted to Caledonian Coal and Goods Depot.

## WESTERN GOODS SHED

A major expansion of the goods yard was undertaken by the GNR between 1897 and 1899. A new Western Goods Shed (an early example of the use of structural steel in buildings) was built on the site of the Coal and Stone Basin in the west of the goods yard (4.9). The canal basin was infilled. The Western Goods Shed was on two levels, with road access from Wharf Road at the upper level and via the coal yard to the lower level. Rail access was also provided to both levels via hydraulic lifts. The adjoining Western Coal Drops were adapted for general goods handling, and the two buildings together now dealt with outward-bound rail traffic, while the Granary complex was adapted to deal solely with incoming rail traffic (8.2, page 95).

The new Outwards Shed had its own first floor suite of offices for clerical staff over the main shed platform and siding space.

## HYDRAULIC POWER

As early as May 1850, Engineer Joseph Cubitt had proposed the purchase of Armstrong hydraulic cranes, which worked initially by hand but ultimately by hydraulic power. High-pressure hydraulic power was in its infancy, led professionally by William Armstrong (1850), and the order for the machinery and accompanying power system was one of the first. A 150,000-gallon (682m$^3$) tank was included on top of the Granary.

Above left: **4.9**: Western Goods Shed viewed from the Regent's Canal at St Pancras Locks, 1911. (Alan Faulkner collection)

Above right: **4.10**: A view of the hydraulic pumping station from the north-east, showing the engine house and accumulator tower; use of hydraulic machinery had ceased sometime earlier, 1976. (Glen Drewett)

Armstrong was to supply twenty 2-ton cranes (shown in 4.3), sixteen 1-ton cranes, eleven sack hoists for the Granary, a steam pumping engine, two locomotive type boilers, three accumulators and all pipework and valves.

A power station was built on the west side of the Granary Basin with, from the south end, the chimney (seen in 4.5), the boiler house, the engine house and the accumulator tower, all of which were adapted to new demands over time. The system was converted to electrical power in 1938, and the chimney and boiler house removed (4.10). From 1958 until the use of hydraulic machinery ended at King's Cross, hydraulic power was purchased from the London Hydraulic Power Company.

On the east side of the Inwards Shed ran the Crane Road, the hydraulic crane being used for heavy loads. Peter Erwood (1988) described very graphically its handling in 1937 of a putrefying whale carcass destined for the Natural History Museum. The Crane Road can be seen in 16.19, page 203.

In 1877 the GNR decided to start replacing horse shunting with use of hydraulic capstans. This led to further investment in such machinery, allowing the Company to save the cost of both horses and manpower. The economics appear finely balanced. An investment of £13,902 was justified as saving eight men and thirty-five horses, which cost the Company upwards of £2,000 a year (£75 per man and £40 per horse) – but interest on investment, maintenance and consumables must have come to almost this amount. A decisive factor could have been the lack of suitable stable accommodation to house ever-increasing numbers of horses.

## WAGONS

The subject of goods wagons could form a separate book, but the purpose here is simply to illustrate a small selection of the enormous variety of wagons that were used by the GNR and its successor, the

LNER (4.11). In addition to those shown, there were open goods wagons, cattle trucks, ballast wagons, rail and sleeper wagons, timber wagons, gunpowder vans, fruit and banana vans and many others (Tatlow, 1998).

## FIRE PROTECTION

Fire was a constant hazard at a goods depot due to a diversity of combustible materials, including hay and straw, oil and grease, timber and sawdust, oily rags and other fibrous materials. These could be ignited by sparks from engines, by lightning, by gas lighting hazards or by spontaneous combustion. Except in the case of lightning, in the event of fire the Company was liable for goods delivered to them for transit. Owing to fire risk, locomotives were not allowed into any of the covered sheds or Potato Market sidings. Wagons were moved by horses or by ropes and hydraulic capstans placed at strategic points around the yard.

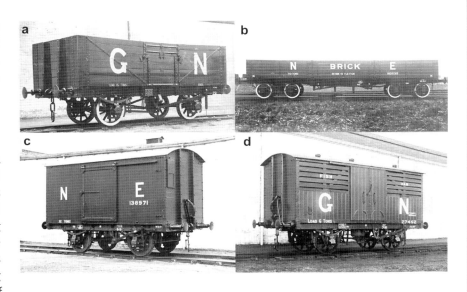

4.11: Goods wagons used by GNR: (a) coal wagon, (b) brick wagon, (c) covered goods wagon, (d) fish wagon. (National Archives)

The absence of certain precautions and appliances for protection against fire resulted in heavy insurance premiums for grain merchants at the Granary, whose complaints prompted the Company into taking measures to reduce the risk and the premiums.

All railway companies faced claims for damage to crops caused by sparks from locomotives, and the GNR – in the drier, cereal-growing east – would have been particularly affected.

The dangers of fire where vigilance was wanting were highlighted at King's Cross underground station in 1987, when a casually discarded match ignited a pile of detritus under an escalator, formed from grease, paper, litter, and fluff, causing a fire that claimed thirty-one lives.

## GOODS WAY

Following the purchase of the gasworks, the Company set about improving the movements of both trains and vehicles. Congreve Street bridge and Battle Bridge Road bridge, at the southern exit of Gasworks Tunnel, were to be removed to allow improvements in the approaches to the passenger station. Somers Bridge was also to be removed and replaced with a new bridge 261ft (80m) to the east (4.12), while Maiden Bridge was to be widened, in agreement with the local authority.

The main improvement was to be a new road on the south side of the canal leading from Wharf Road at its junction with Cambridge Street to York Road (4.12). Small parcels of land were exchanged with the Regent's Canal Company, which led to the wharf frontage at the former gasworks being realigned. The new bridge over the canal (which later became Excel Bridge) was to link the roadway

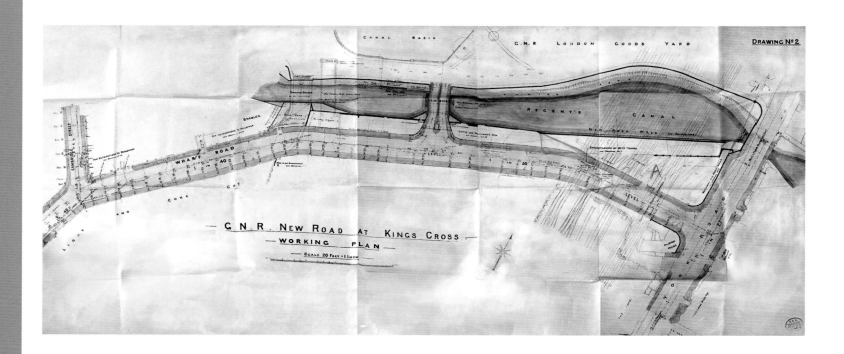

**4.12**: A new road at King's Cross: the plan for Goods Way, August 1917. (National Archives)

on the north side off the canal to the new road on the south side, thereby relieving chronic traffic congestion caused by coal traffic from Cambridge Street having to cross Somers Bridge, and compete with the traffic to and from the Outwards and Inwards Sheds.

Powers to execute these works were obtained in 1913 but little was done before the end of the First World War. By then a further decision had been taken to improve circulation: the filling of Granary Basin. No additional powers were needed for this work, which continued intermittently from 1915.

In 1918 Sir Robert McAlpine was contracted to build the new road. It was initially named Wharf Road, as an extension of the road that had led to Somers Bridge, but was renamed Goods Way in 1921. The name Wharf Road was then given to the road, previously unnamed, that led from York Road into the goods yard on the north side of Regent's Canal. Access into the goods yard was controlled from a small brick gatehouse on the south side, adjoining Goods Way.

The new arrangement finally allowed carters to bypass the steep approach to the goods yard when crossing Maiden Lane Bridge, which had been a source of trouble for more than sixty years.

# Locomotive Sheds

# five

## LAYOUT AND FUNCTION OF THE LOCOMOTIVE DEPOT

When first established, the Locomotive Depot, subsequently known as Top Shed, was the furthest north of the facilities in the goods yard. Later the area between the depot and the NLR became a coal stacking ground, and was filled with sidings. The plan in 5.1 shows the depot at its peak in 1906, with the Midland Railway main line to St Pancras forming the western boundary. At this time there were three locomotive sheds in the Top Shed area: the Erecting Shed, the Running Shed and the Midland Roundhouse – as well as the Passenger Locomotive Shed, known as Bottom Shed, at King's Cross Station.

King's Cross depot carried out heavy repairs and locomotive overhaul for the first fifty years of its life, but when this work switched to Doncaster it reverted to more routine repairs to locomotives, which it continued to perform until the depot closed.

The depot could be reached on foot by the perimeter road, Wharf Road, and the first building reached on the south side was the Locomotive Office, where staff would sign on.

**5.1**: The Locomotive Depot: an extract from the 1906 GNR plan. (British Railways/ David Millbank Challis collections)

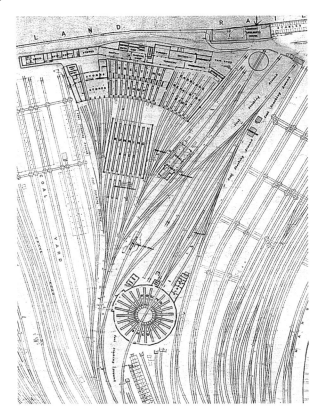

## ORIGINAL LOCOMOTIVE SHED (ERECTING SHED)

The locomotive shed built in 1850–51 was a crescent-shaped building that provided twenty-five roads, each individually served, as shown in 5.2 and 5.3. The area outside the front of the shed was for servicing locomotives and for other shed work in the open; no coking facilities appear to have been provided.

As shown in 5.4, there was an eleven-road repair shop in the middle section with a series of shops behind that were responsible for repairing carriages, wagons and carts as well as engines. The Smithy was also responsible for shoeing horses. A 40ft turntable was provided near Maiden Lane. It was moved in 1855 to allow development of the Potato Market and a second turntable was requested by Archibald Sturrock (Locomotive Engineer 1850–66) in 1855 to avoid tender-first working.

A large part of the original 1850 building remained in use for engine repairs until the depot closed in 1963.

**5.2**: Original Locomotive Shed or Erecting Shed, *c*.1851. (CLSAC)

**5.3**: Locomotive Hall, early 1850s, which later became the Back Erecting Shop, here used for preparation and servicing. The separation of tenders from locomotives reflected an early shortage of tenders. (CLSAC)

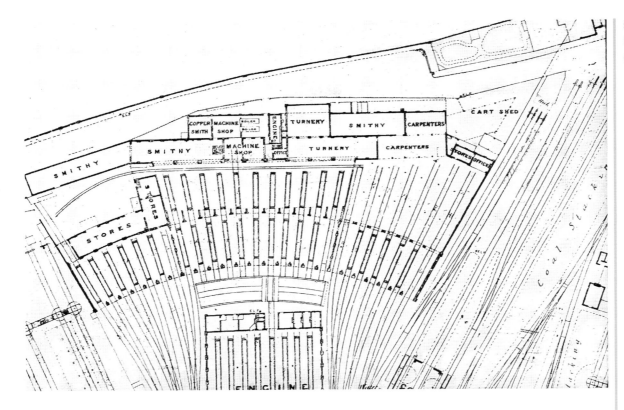

# MAIN LINE RUNNING SHED

By 1861, the original engine stables were becoming inadequate for accommodating the number of locomotives allocated. Construction of a new engine shed, the Main Line Running Shed, was combined with moving the carriage repair facilities from the passenger station and with provision of additional repair facilities, as shown in 5.4. The new shed, seen from the side in 5.5, was built immediately in front of the 1850 engine stables. One of the eight parallel roads was taken through the back of the shed onto a traverser that allowed engines to be positioned on any one of eight roads in the original Erecting Shed.

The eleven tracks originally provided for repair and overhaul of locomotives continued to be used for this purpose, leading into the Front Erecting Shop, which had been provided with a higher roof, as can be seen in 5.6. It connected with the other shops – smithies, machine shops, carpenters, turnery and coppersmiths – and was served by an overhead travelling crane.

The seven shorter roads at the south end became the Paint and Carpenter's Shop, while the seven at the north end, extended in length in 1862, were made into the Carriage and Wagon Repair Shop.

The repair shops provided generous accommodation for blacksmiths (5.7). A further smithy was provided in the stables complex to the north to service a large and growing stud. A shop in the north-west corner of the depot provided for the repair of road carts. Opposite this on the perimeter road was the Locomotive Superintendent's house and garden. Unlike the Running Shed, this survived the closure of the Locomotive Depot until it also went in about 2001 to clear the route for the Channel Tunnel Rail Link (CTRL).

The front or eastern end of the Running Shed, with water tank, is shown in 5.8. The curved front of the Erecting Shed can be seen behind on the left. In a 1931 photograph of the Running Shed (5.9), the hoist has been removed and the coaling plant can be seen on the right, shortly before it was replaced by a mechanical coaling plant.

Top: **5.5**: The Running Shed: shed staff with Sturrock and Stirling tank engines. (Ian Allen Library)

Above: **5.6**: The Front Erecting Shop, 1927. (SSPL/NRM)

## MIDLAND ROUNDHOUSE

Built to serve the Midland Railway, the Roundhouse was completed in February 1859, one year after the MR had started passenger services into King's Cross. It was provided with its own coking and watering facilities. It featured a 40ft (12m) diameter central turntable from which twenty-four roads radiated (5.10). Four engine pits were initially provided, with seven more added in 1862.

Above left: **5.7**: The Blacksmith's Shop. (SSPL/NRM)

Above right: **5.9**: The Running Shed with the Coaling Plant, 1931, C.C.B. Herbert. (SSPL/NRM)

Left: **5.8**: The Running Shed in 1913, H.C. Casserley. (R.M. Casserley collection)

The shed was taken over by the GNR when the MR vacated it in 1868, requiring additional engine pits and providing accommodation for their own locomotives, mainly tank engines. It was demolished in 1931 as part of a programme of improvements.

## PASSENGER LOCOMOTIVE DEPOT

A small carriage repair shop had been built at King's Cross station in 1853, but this was converted into an engine shed for six locomotives with a turntable in 1862, and the carriage repair facilities were removed to the Erecting Shed. The engine shed survived until 1876, when it made way for new suburban platforms. A new engine shed was built further west, with turntable, workshops and coaling stage, separated from the Suburban Station by a long brick wall.

The new station once again fell victim to Suburban Station expansion westwards in about 1893, a taller brick wall being built to support the new Suburban Station roof. This wall can be seen in 5.11, with the passenger loco squeezed into the space between the wall and the Hotel Curve, the coaling stage being prominent. On the western side of the Hotel Curve lay Platform 16.

After the GNR had acquired part of the Imperial Gasworks site and removed Congreve Street, which bridged the tracks south of Gasworks Tunnel, it constructed a new road, Goods Way, over the top of Gasworks Tunnel in 1918, as described in the last chapter. This allowed the removal of Battle Bridge Road and the excavation of the former gasworks canal basin as a site for the Passenger Locomotive Depot (5.12), which was relocated from the station in 1923, enabling new platforms 14 and 15 to be built on the former locomotive yard site (3.11). A new 70ft (21m) diameter turntable was provided (5.13), being completed in 1924, which allowed the larger engines to be turned at King's Cross rather than having to make the round trip to Ferme Park Yard.

Below left: **5.10**: Midland Roundhouse, showing wooden smoke chutes and turntable decking. Some tender engines share the pits with suburban tank engines, *c*. 1910. (P.N. Townend collection)

Below right: **5.11**: The King's Cross Passenger Locomotive Depot with the Hotel Curve, as seen in the August 1914 edition of *Railway Magazine*. (ICE)

# MOVE OR IMPROVE – LATER ALTERATIONS

In January 1882, the General Manager, Henry Oakley, noted that congestion in the goods yard was becoming acute and costing the company in extra shunting. He advised the Board:

> Looking therefore at the necessity for further room in the goods yard and to the almost equal necessity for further accommodation for the Locomotive Department, it appears to be necessary to contemplate the removal of the Locomotive Department from its present site, and utilise the space thus gained for the purpose of relieving the pressure of our goods and coal traffic.

Nevertheless, after an inspection by the Board he was able to propose a temporary and much cheaper solution that deferred any decision on relocating the Locomotive Department: converting the Coal Stacking Ground in the northern part of the site into goods sidings.

The traverser between the Running Shed and the Erecting Shed appears to have been removed in about 1906. In the same year plans were prepared showing how the Running Shed could be extended and the original Erecting Shed could be used as a running shed, filling up the hole occupied by the traverser. Seven of the eight tracks were extended through into the Erecting Shop, where previously a single track had served the traverser and the Repair Shop.

In 1911 a plant was provided for washing out locomotive boilers with hot water at the Running Shed.

In 1929 the Traffic Committee once again looked at the rearrangement of the depot as the stabling accommodation was proving inadequate and movement of engines costly and difficult. Accommodation was wanted for 200 engines. The solution depended on moving the work of the carriage repairing shop to Highgate and converting the vacated site into a locomotive shed for seventeen-tank engines that would take the place of the Midland Roundhouse, which would be demolished. The major improvements were:

- additional roads with more examination pits
- a mechanical coaling plant with two bunkers of 250 tons capacity, and the necessary siding capacity for full and empty coal wagons
- ash pits with sunk ash wagon road for better removal of ashes
- a 70ft (21m) turntable to replace the existing 52ft (16m) table
- a modern sand drying plant.

Below: **5.12**: The Passenger Locomotive Depot, 1952. (Irwell Press)

A further improvement was the construction of a new water-softening plant, located at the south end of the locomotive offices. This allowed the water supply to revert to the Regent's Canal, a cheaper source than mains water, and reduced the formation of hard scale and corrosion in boilers. Most of these works were carried out in 1931–32 and were complete by the mid-1930s; thereafter little further alteration was made. The increasing length of locomotives did not allow as many as planned to be accommodated at Top Shed. The allocation listed for 1958 was 125 steam and 23 diesel.

## WORK ON STEAM LOCOMOTIVES

Maintenance of steam locomotives was highly labour-intensive, requiring an army of men that the Company separated into a multitude of grades. After several hours working, the intense heat in a boiler caused the solids and ash content of coal to fuse and form thick solids called 'clinker' on the fire bars, preventing oxygen from reaching the fire and thereby reducing steam pressure. Spent fuel in the form of ash settled in the smokebox under the chimney to quite a depth, which had to be emptied after every run – a very dirty job.

On arrival at the depot via Five Arch, drivers reported to the office near the turntable for instructions, before proceeding onto the turntable (5.14). After turning they continued to the coaling plant (5.15). This had two hoppers, allowing different grades of coal to be separated. Harder coal was generally used for main line locomotives, while local work used a lower grade. Welsh coal was generally too soft for such mechanical plants.

Right: **5.13**: *Flying Scotsman* on the 70ft (21m) turntable in the Passenger Locomotive Depot, 1928. The corridor in the tender allowed the driver and fireman to be relieved during the run without a stop being necessary. (Mary Evans)

Far right: **5.15:** New England's Thompson Class A2 Pacific No. 60513 *Dante* is coaled up for a return journey north on 9 May 1954. (Brian Morrison)

THE KING'S CROSS STORY: 200 YEARS OF HISTORY IN THE RAILWAY LANDS

After being coaled, locomotives moved onto the ash pits alongside the coal hopper (5.16). Firedropping was carried out by staff paid on a bonus system. The fire would be cleaned by withdrawal from the firebox with a long steel shovel and thrown onto the ground. With freight engine fireboxes typically of 28 sq. ft ($2.6m^2$), filled with fire up to 2ft (0.6m) deep, this was a long, dangerous and dirty job, made easier when LNER engines had drop grates. Wooden clogs were a standard issue. On leaving the ash pit area an engine's sandboxes were replenished with dry sand. Locomotives were then moved into either of the two Running Sheds or onto the Back Pits. Locomotives that needed to be ready for their next workings immediately were placed in the Back Pits, where they were prepared and watered in the open. The Back Pits had been built on the site of the old Midland Roundhouse and consisted of seven straight roads. Here locomotives would be given a general check by an Examining Fitter, who was usually equipped with a long wheel-tapping hammer.

Following any repairs arising from the examination, the locomotive was then ready for the engine crew to prepare it for its next working by making up the fire, trimming the coal, oiling around the engine and watering.

In 1900 six summonses had been issued against the Company by the London County Council because of nuisance caused by smoke from engines. Later, a variety of techniques were used to avoid the problems of steam raising, which became an increasing issue from 1956 under the Clean Air Act. A firebox powder or briquette placed on the fire could turn black smoke white for long enough to satisfy visiting Local Authority inspectors, but the major strategy was to work closely with such inspectors so that they could experience the problems for themselves.

Above left: **5.14**: On the turntable in the Locomotive Depot, 1948, H.C. Casserley. (R.M. Casserley collection)

Above right: **5.16**: Sidings with the mechanical coaling plant and ashpits, looking east from the top of the water-softening plant towards Five Arch and York Way 1956. (SSPL/NRM)

# Horse Power

# six

## COMPETITION WITH MAN AND MACHINE

Victorian London remained dependent on horses for the movement of goods and people despite the steam engine taking over ever more functions. Horses were so fundamental a power source that their service life became a business decision. Robert Bakewell, the best-known breeder of the eighteenth century, had sought to discover the animal that was the best machine for turning food into money. The mid-century Victorian attitude was expressed as 'sentiment pays no dividend': the horse had to earn its place as a source of power in competition with both man and machine.

At the beginning of the nineteenth century, the cost of keeping a horse was two to three times the hire of a day labourer, while the daily work of a horse was equal to that of five or six men. The cost of horse power was therefore about half that of manpower. It was reduced further over the next century, while the cost of manpower increased.

The horse's advantage over the machine started with low cost and flexibility, but as machines became more powerful, the horse had to work harder to compete. Competition led to an increase in the size of horses, an increase in the horse's workload, and a reduced working life. This trend was manifested by a US tram company that depreciated its horses at 7 per cent in 1880 and 16 per cent in 1885. This accountancy measure reduced a fifteen-year working life to six years.

The weight of streetcar (tram) horses in the USA increased by 50 per cent between 1860 and 1880, allowing fewer horses per car. New York 'street railway' companies experimented with light steam-powered vehicles, but by 1870 these had been given up as too costly, the animal triumphing over the machine – with some help from regulation.

## EQUINE DUTIES

The movement of higher value goods to both national destinations and to and from the ports was largely in the hands of the railway companies. Railways were the major users of horses prior to the First World War and needed a variety of working horses.

While the heavier tasks such as shunting were typically undertaken by Shire horses and Clydesdales (6.1), the great majority of horses in railway company stables comprised heavy horses for goods cartage and half-heavies or 'vanners' for faster parcels and passenger luggage duties.

In addition to the railway companies, several other companies and individuals were involved in the carrying trade. The largest of these, Pickford & Co. and Carter Paterson, had some 4,000 and 2,000 horses respectively towards the end of the century. In total, the metropolitan carrying trade amounted to some 25,000 horses, about 10 per cent of all the horses and ponies that were estimated to be working in London at the end of the nineteenth century.

At King's Cross, 70–80 per cent of horses employed by the GNR were used in the goods yard for cartage. Parcels horses, most working out of the Passenger Stables, made up some 10–15 per cent. Until the 1880s, about 10 per cent of horses were employed in shunting. This fell to near zero by the end of the century, as by then almost all shunting used hydraulic power. The decline of the shunting horse was offset by the rise of the omnibus horse as railway companies increasingly undertook the transfer of passengers between railway termini.

Just like the motor car in the twentieth century, the horse was a potent symbol of social status both in town and in the country. The ease of travel on the railways enabled the wealthier classes to work in town and enjoy hunting at weekends. They supported some 200,000 hunters outside the metropolis, which itself created a strong demand for horse transport on the railways.

## GNR STUD AT KING'S CROSS

Horse power was as indispensable as locomotive power for the operations of the railway and occupied a comparable amount of management time. Horse numbers at King's Cross were the responsibility of the Horse Committee, and before this the Executive and Traffic Committee, which made recommendations to the Board with the support of the General Manager. The Board approved the 'stud', as the number of horses employed by the GNR was known, and this was divided between London and Country, and further divided within London between King's Cross and other depots.

Based on the available data, an estimate can be made of the growth of the approved stud allocated to King's Cross from 1850 to 1910. The graphical presentation (6.2) shows a steady rise in numbers until the mid-1890s when horse numbers may have dipped below what was required, only to be over-provided in the next few years with a peak in 1900 of about 1,300 according to Wade (1900).

The anomaly in the 1890s appears to be related to a critical report in 1895 by Professor J. Wortley Axe of the Royal Veterinary College. Responding to a severe outbreak of influenza, he recommended better stable accommodation and the separation of sick and injured horses. His recommendations led to substantial new building, both new stables and raising of some existing stables to two or three floors.

The GN preferred to buy seasoned horses, that is horses at 7 years old that had been sold by the breeder and broken in, usually through work on farms near urban centres. But it became increasingly difficult to find such horses, and the Company was compelled to buy 5-year-olds and put them into work. Unseasoned horses incurred greater risk of sickness and would be placed in 'Reception', separated from the main stud while their duties were gradually increased.

The Horse Department of the Company tried to maintain a good stud available for all emergencies, and pleaded for moderate loads, low speed and general good usage. They tried to keep about

**6.1**: Horsepower in the Shunting Yard, oil on canvas, undated, David Shepherd. (courtesy of Avril Shepherd)

**6.2**: GNR-approved stud at King's Cross.

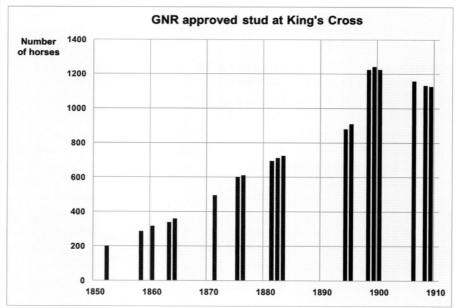

THE KING'S CROSS STORY: 200 YEARS OF HISTORY IN THE RAILWAY LANDS

one-third of the stud at 'rest' or as 'exchange horses' and 'horses in course of seasoning to their work'. The Traffic Department, on the other hand, sought to get as much work as every horse could fairly stand, and objected to being charged for more than a certain percentage of horses over and above those working daily with the vans.

There was always a proportion of the stud that was sick or injured, or convalescing from sickness and injury, and hence off-duty. In the 1880s, this amounted to about 10 per cent of the total, a higher figure than the GN's competitors, which was attributed to working practices. Improvements in these and in stabling appear to have brought it down to about 5 per cent by 1900.

Railway horses would typically have a working life of four to six years, before being sold on. In the 1890s a horse cost about £50, somewhat lower than in earlier periods. The cost was depreciated at 20 per cent per year, which suggests that at the end of a six-year working life for the railway the horse was worth about 25 per cent of its purchase cost.

## THE VICTORIAN WORKING HORSE STABLE

Stables need to provide light and dry bedding, a modest space, ventilation without draughts, and good drainage. Yet the Victorian working horse was kept at ground level or 'below grade', often in poor or makeshift conditions, such as within railway arches or in the basements of warehouses. Stabling of horses on well-aired and well-lit upper floors accessible by ramps appears not to have been tried in London before about 1870.

Stables typically consisted of an access passage and stalls on one or both sides. A standard size stall was about 6ft 2in (1.88m) wide, separated from its neighbour either by a partition or by a swing bale, a heavy wood section strung on chains from the rafters. Both forms of division are shown in 6.3, alternating along the two sides.

A standard length of stall was 10ft (3.05m) with a passage of 8–10ft (2.4–3.0m). The stable shown (6.3) is 28ft (8.5m) wide overall, typical of the larger GNR stables. A central passage slopes to drains on each side, and roof trusses are supported by timber posts that align with solid stall partitions. There are also various hooks and pegs for harnesses, collars and tackle, each horse having its dedicated and identified equipment.

Larger stalls or loose boxes stabled horses needing to recover from injury or illness. Loose boxes were typically 15ft (4.6m) by 12ft (3.7m).

Much of the GNR's provision of stable accommodation failed to keep up with improvements in stable space, ventilation, light and drainage that were being promoted in the fourth quarter of the nineteenth century. Accommodation for sick and lame horses proved inadequate and was often under strain, coming

6.3: The interior of Great Northern Stables on Blundell Street, from *Railway Magazine*, 1900, Vol. 8. (ICE)

to a head in 1890 with a serious outbreak of influenza. However, many improvements followed over the next few years – the decision in 1897 to provide a large new stable at Blundell Street, close to Copenhagen Tunnel, should be seen in this context.

## STABLE ACCOMMODATION AT KING'S CROSS

The steady increase in the stud created a need for stable accommodation that the GNR often struggled to meet, eventually involving fragmentation into some fifteen to twenty separate stables in the King's Cross area. Despite Joseph Cubitt, the engineer, enjoining that stables be placed 'reasonably near to those parts of the Station where the horses are most wanted, vizt [sic] the Goods warehouse and Coal depot', there was ultimately little space for stables except at the periphery of the Railway Lands. Summary information about the various stables provided in about 1910 at King's Cross is given in the table opposite.

The first stables to be built were indeed centrally located: those in the basements of the two Transit Sheds and the Coal Stables in the arches of the viaduct under Wharf Road (6.4), together providing accommodation for about 270 horses. Recent photographs show the semi-spiral ramp to the Eastern Transit Shed Stable (6.5), which was approached from the internal roadway, and the passage connecting the arches of the former Coal Stables (6.6). Both Transit Shed approach ramps have been re-buried after recording.

These earliest stables were followed by the Parcels Stables in Edmund Street at King's Cross Station and a series of stables ranges in the north-west corner of the yard, beyond the Locomotive Sheds (6.7), which included the Hospital Stables complex that served a wider area than King's Cross. Photographs of the Hospital Stables complex from about 1900 are shown in 6.8 and 6.9.

Given the numbers of horses working in the goods yard and collecting/delivering goods, it is certain that other horses were stabled off-site either by the agents that worked for the railway company or by the railway company itself, or both.

The Traffic Committee in 1897 recommended construction of stabling for the accommodation of 190 horses alongside the Copenhagen Tunnel, at a cost of £13,680 (about £1.4 million in present purchasing power). The new stable in Blundell Street was visited by a journalist, George Wade, in 1900, who wrote in glowing terms of the treatment of horses by the GNR. The layout of the stables is shown in 6.10, and the arrangement of stalls in one of the stable ranges is shown in 6.3.

The fabric of the five former stable range buildings on the north side of the stable yard remains largely as it was when they were stables (6.11).

## HORSE KEEPING

The cost of keeping a horse in 1908 was 19.5 shillings per week for the GNR, or £50 per year, equivalent in present purchasing power to about £5,000 a year. The running cost over a year was therefore comparable to the purchase price.

## King's Cross Stables c.1910

| Location | Name(s) | Built | Stalls | Description/comment |
|---|---|---|---|---|
| Transit Sheds/ Granary forecourt | Eastern Transit Shed Inwards Shed Market Stable | 1851 | 78 | In the basement of Eastern Transit Shed occupying 280ft (86m) by 28ft (8.6m) approximately, with spiral ramps down from roadway. Granite-sett floor, and brick jack-arched ceiling on cast-iron beams and columns to support the platforms. Not equipped as stables until 1852. Emergency exit provided in case of fire in 1898. |
| | Western Transit Shed Outwards Shed Shunting Stable | 1851 | 77 | As above, but in basement of Western Transit Shed; accommodated horses 'of the largest type'. Exit passage to additional stabling in Eastern Coal Drops. Further exit sanctioned 1899. |
| | Provender Stable | 1854 | 70 | Initially (1854) a building for storing and preparing horse provender, to which sidings were laid in 1856. Became a stable for twenty-six horses in basement (1860); proposals for stabling further ninety-five horses on two floors above Yard level with ramp, but would seem impossible that there were more than seventy overall on three floors. |
| Wharf Road and Cambridge Street Coal Drops | Coal Stables | 1851 | 154 | In 24 low arches under Wharf Road extending over a length of about 500ft (150m), following the bend in the canal. Depth of arches varied from about 28ft (8.6m) in northwest to about 45ft (14m) in southeast. Communicated via a central passage, most arches giving standing to six horses; ventilated by openings on canal side. Initially 120 stalls provided for Edward Wiggins, Contractor for Delivery of Coals, but extended in 1897. |
| | Wiggins Stables | 1861 | 145 | Opposite Coal and Fish Offices along Regent's Canal. Single storey in six ranges, with accommodation for 108 horses; later raised to two storeys. Included sheds and offices. Was built and occupied by Silkstone & Elsecar Coal Owner's Company until 1882 when it was acquired by GNR. |
| | Tozer's Stables | ? | 40 | Separated from Wiggins Stables by Van Yard. Two floors with ramp, removed 1901 from outside to inside of the stables. |
| Hospital Infirmary Complex (northwest corner of goods depot) | New Stable | 1854 | 115 | Initially comprised a stable range and granary for Edward Wiggins, the Coals cartage contractor, with accommodation for sixty horses. Raised to two floors 1897 for additional fifty-four horses. |
| | Convalescent Stable Hospital Stables | 1854 | 90 | Long range of stabling adjoining the hospital yard. Had stall accommodation on the ground floor for seventy-six. Raised in 1890s to two floors with thirty loose boxes. |
| | Horse Infirmary | 1853 | 13 loose boxes | The complex included thirteen loose boxes, six isolation boxes, straw yard, a horse pond and two cottages, one for the man in charge of the Horse Infirmary Complex. |
| | Midland Stables | 1858 | 120 | Seven separate enclosures providing stalls for sixty-two horses, initially stabling horses of Midland Co. Taken over by the GNR after the Midland vacated the goods yard in 1862. Additional floor for sixty horses provided c. 1891. Later became 'Reception' Stables, suitable for separating new horses from remainder of stock. |
| | One Horse Van Stables | 1872 | 45 | On single floor. |
| | New Wagon Stable Wagon Horse Stable | 1866 | 107 | Initially at ground level for sixty horses. First floor added 1898 for further forty-seven horses with two ramps and an emergency exit. |
| | Shoeing Shop Smithy | c1862 | | In three sections. Western section is five bays, central section seven bays and eastern section two bays. Inverted hipped roof channelled noxious fumes to high-level vents on sides for expelling air. Low-level vents allowed fresh air to enter. |
| Edmund Street north side, west of Passenger Station | Parcels Cart stables Passenger Stables Nag Horse Stables | 1853 | About 90 | Built by John Jay. Extended by conversion of laundry for Great Northern Hotel. George Wade (1900) estimated 185 working in Parcels Section and forty on omnibus duty. On two floors with inclined roadway to upper floor. |
| Northeast areas | Arch Stable | 1881 | 23 | Two arches below the Maiden Lane viaduct, arranged as stables, originally for Kilner Bros. |
| | Blundell Street Stables | 1898 | 180 | Two sets of stable ranges forming an angle that enclosed a stable yard. The northern stables comprised five ranges, typically with eight horses in stalls each side of a central passage. Southern stables about 420ft (128m) long, divided into five bays, four with twenty-four horses in stalls, the fifth with seven loose boxes. |

**6.4**: The central complex of stables, extracted from the 1906 GNR plan overlaid by author. (British Railways/ David Millibank Challis collections)

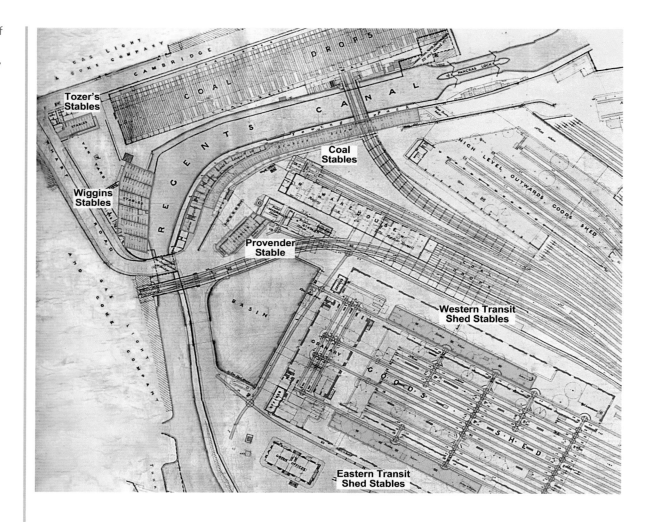

The breakdown by cost category is shown in on page 82 in graph 6.12. Depreciation, the second largest item, represented only one-sixth of the cost of horse keep. By far the largest item was provender (feed), which accounted for more than half the cost: a horse consumed about 1.4 tons of oats and 2.4 tons of hay each year. Maize had largely replaced oats for many duties by 1875. The fodder market represented over 10 per cent of agricultural output by the end of the nineteenth century, with London by far the largest market in the country. As transport costs fell, and with the arrival of baling presses to reduce bulk for transport, sources of supply expanded as far as the Americas.

The GNR built spacious provender stores at Holloway for its London stud in the 1880s, with full facilities for cutting, blending and sacking. This took the pressure off the increasingly inadequate Provender Stores at King's Cross, enabling their subsequent conversion into stabling.

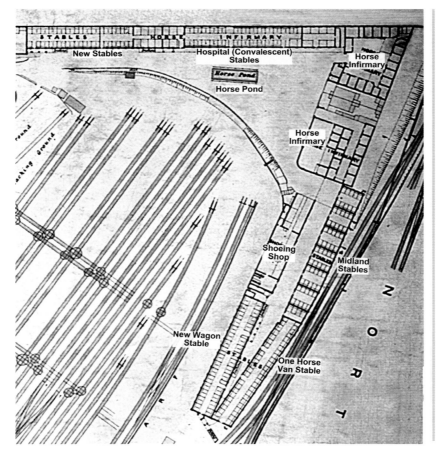

Above left: **6.5**: The semi-spiral approach ramp to the stables under the Eastern Transit Shed. (Argent)

Above right: **6.6**: The view along the central passage of stabling under Wharf Road; the arches were being used to store artefacts recovered from recent excavations. (Argent)

Left: **6.7**: A plan of the stables in the north-west corner of yard, extracted from the 1906 GNR plan overlaid by author. (British Railways/David Millibank Challis collections)

Above left: **6.8**: Hospital (Convalescent) Stables, *c*.1900. (C. Pilkington)

Above right: **6.9**: Horse Bathing at the GNR Hospital, *c*.1900. (C. Pilkington)

## WARHORSE

The British had long been indifferent to the importance of horses for defence, unlike their Continental neighbours. Not until 1920 did stallions require licences, by which time the horse was no longer vital for war.

The War Office did, however, instigate a voluntary registration of horses for the army. The GNR registered 100 of the company's horses for military service when required, receiving an annual payment of 10 shillings per horse.

The army had 25,000 horses at the start of the First World War, out of a civilian pool of nearly 4 million in Britain and Ireland. It quickly impressed an extra 140,000. Within twelve months it had over 500,000 on active service, about half recruited from America, where mechanisation had depressed prices. However, much of the UK pool proved below army standards, as the more powerful bus and tram horses were almost extinct by 1914.

## TENACITY OF HORSE CARTAGE

By the early twentieth century, street space occupied by horse-drawn vehicles was causing insupportable congestion and threatened traffic paralysis. The horseless carriage was a direct substitute for the horse, occupying at least 25 per cent less space. Nevertheless, owing to lack of confidence in motor vehicle technology and its cost advantages, legislative initiatives were required to drive horses off the streets.

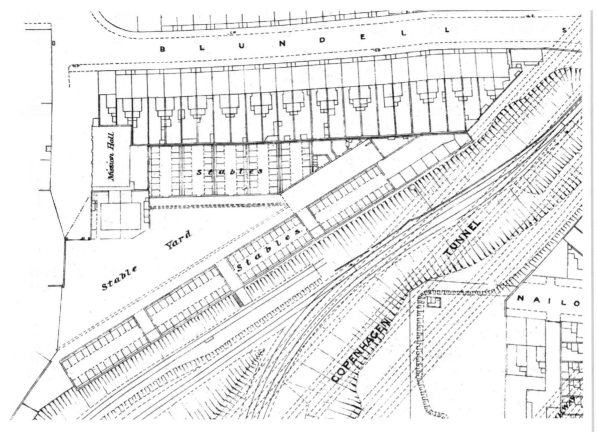

**6.10**: The plan of Great Northern Stables in Blundell Street, 1900. (MRC Collection)

Buses, trams and cabs, where convenience, speed and comfort outweighed costs and flexibility, rapidly adopted the new technology. But shifting the horse from railway duties proved a slow business (6.13). The infrastructure for horse cartage was already in place and replacement of horses and carts competed with other uses for scarce capital. The costs were low for maintaining horse-drawn vehicles, while motor vehicles in the 1930s were costly, even when the LNER fitted its own bodies to the chassis. While the carter was on his morning round, a second cart would be loaded for afternoon deliveries. By contrast, motor vehicles were idle while loading.

A horse's low top speed was less of a disadvantage in areas with traffic congestion. In 1938 motor lorries were restricted to 30mph, 20mph if articulated or over 2.5 tons loaded.

The internal combustion engine finally signed the death warrant of the working horse after the Second World War: in 1947–48 more than 200,000 horses were put down, 40 per cent under 3 years old.

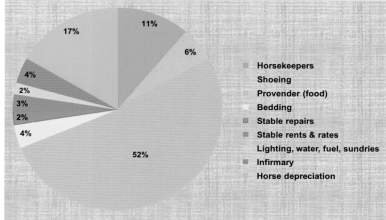

- Horsekeepers
- Shoeing
- Provender (food)
- Bedding
- Stable repairs
- Stable rents & rates
- Lighting, water, fuel, sundries
- Infirmary
- Horse depreciation

11% 6% 52% 4% 2% 3% 2% 4% 17%

**Above left: 6.11**: Three of the former Great Northern Stables ranges in Blundell Street, 2016. (Peter Darley)

**Above right: 6.12**: The relative cost components of horse keep in 1908. (RAIL 236/395/17, National Archives)

**Right: 6.13**: The tenacity of railway cartage in the face of the general decline in horse-drawn traffic. (Sources as shown)

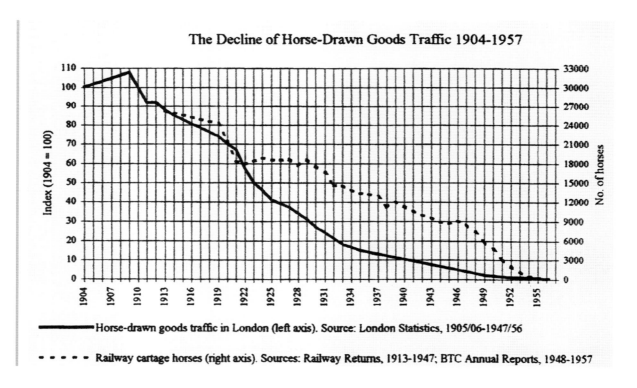

### The Decline of Horse-Drawn Goods Traffic 1904-1957

Horse-drawn goods traffic in London (left axis). Source: London Statistics, 1905/06-1947/56

- - - - - Railway cartage horses (right axis). Sources: Railway Returns, 1913-1947; BTC Annual Reports, 1948-1957

# Coal Supply

# seven

## DEMAND AND SUPPLY

When the King's Cross goods station opened, the trade in coal imported into London had reached about 3.5 million tons. Almost all was seaborne. Twenty years later, in 1871, this trade had doubled to over 7 million tons, with railways having captured over 60 per cent (Simmons, 1986). A further fifteen years later, in a letter to *The Times*, Firth (1886) referred to over 11 million tons coming into the London coal tax area yearly, of which nearly 7 million came by railway. The rail-borne quantity did not change greatly over the next twenty years.

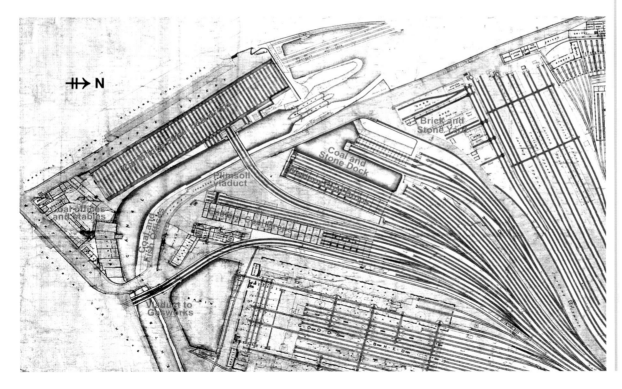

**7.1**: A plan of coal facilities, an extract from the 1895 GNR plan overlaid by author. (P.N. Townend/David Millibank Challis collections)

According to Gordon (1893), Londoners each burned an average of about a ton of coal annually, so that London residents burned 5 million tons a year at the turn of the century. Gas companies used about 3 million tons per year. At that time, total London traffic was about 14 million tons, which leaves industry consuming about 6 million tons. Much of this would have powered the steamships bunkered in the port of London and locomotives carrying passengers and freight to and from the capital.

The GNR set out to capture a significant part of the coal trade and King's Cross was the first great coal depot set up by a railway company for the supply of what was an indispensable mineral to the metropolis.

However, 100 years later, in the 1950s and 1960s, the demand for coal declined drastically, both domestically and industrially. Not only were more and more deliveries being made by road, but the Clean Air Act and the development of North Sea gas were having a major impact, with activity in the Railway Lands reflecting this.

## KING'S CROSS COAL DEPOT – FEATURES AND CHRONOLOGY

King's Cross Coal Depot was established on the north and east sides of the Regent's Canal (7.1). Joseph Cubitt considered that the coal facilities established in 1851, the Eastern Coal Drops and the Coal and Stone Basin, were capable of handling 1,000 tons a day. The latter had a dock of about 200 x 35ft (61 x 11m) for coal traffic on the south side of the basin, and another 125 x 50ft (38 x 15m) for stone traffic on the north side. Beyond the basin to the north, sidings and warehouses for brick and stone were built in 1854. Despite the association of coal with brick and stone as 'minerals', we shall address the brick and stone trade in the next chapter.

The Western Coal Drops were completed in 1860 alongside the Coal and Stone Basin, where there had previously been coal staithes (i.e. coal drops) to serve barges, with a timber viaduct separating the basin from the coal drops. The coal staithes were moved to the opposite (north) side of the southern arm of the basin, and in 1863 were converted to 'tumbling platforms', similar to those in use on the NLR, whereby the coal was more quickly unloaded.

The Coal and Fish Offices were started in 1852. Until 1860, the GNR was trading coal on its own account and worked with a single contractor for coal delivery, providing him with stabling, office, granary and hay store. In 1860 a Chancery suit compelled the GN to cease such trading, and it sold or hired out its wagons, vans and sacks to other coal traders, whom it was now obliged to accommodate. The Coal and Fish Offices were therefore enlarged in 1860, and the Company appropriated the offices in the Western Transit Shed of Edward Wiggins, the former coal delivery contractor.

In 1864 the Western Coal Drops were provided with additional lines of rails to remove empty wagons. This proved successful and was adopted for the Eastern Coal Drops, which were provided with a viaduct and traverser for manoeuvring of empty wagons in 1865.

Land at Cambridge Street was acquired from the Ecclesiastical Commissioners by Samuel Plimsoll (inventor of the Plimsoll line for ships) for coal drops in 1864. The next year, houses, stables and canal-side wharves were cleared for the erection of a viaduct that brought the railway across the canal

Above left: **7.2**: A coal train awaiting entry into the Metropolitan Tunnel at York Road Station, for onward transport to railway companies south of the river, *c.*1925. (Irwell Press)

Above right: **7.3**: Coal barged on Regent's Canal near Hanover Lodge. (CRT)

Left: **7.4**: A cart in A.J. Salter's coal merchants' yard on Cambridge (Camley) Street, with a railway wagon on the traverser above and gas holders, 1945–50, John Gay. (Historic England)

to Plimsoll's coal depot on the west side of the canal. The first coal was consigned to Samuel Plimsoll's sidings in July 1866. Further pieces of land were bought from the Ecclesiastical Commissioners in April 1868 and used to extend the coal drops. This allowed the first coal to be barged from Cambridge Street in June that year. Little coal was barged after 1893.

In 1867 a viaduct was constructed across the Regent's Canal to serve the Imperial Gas Light and Coke Company. The first coal consigned to the gasworks was delivered in January 1868 and consignments continued until the gasworks ceased to manufacture gas in 1904.

During 1875–76 the southern part of the Eastern Coal Drops were converted into five warehouses to meet a demand for accommodation from traders using the London Station. The first block was let to Bagley, Wild & Co., a bottle manufacturer.

In 1891 the GN Company purchased the Cambridge Street Coal Drops from Samuel Plimsoll's heirs. They gradually extended the coal drops up to Wharf Road over the decade 1896 to 1905 and added offices for coal merchants, partly in response to large extensions made by the Midland Company to their Somers Town Depot.

In 1897–99 the Western Coal Drops were converted to become part of the Western Goods Shed, a two-level warehouse for outwards goods built over the Coal and Stone Basin, which was infilled. At the same time, the Plimsoll Viaduct was rebuilt in iron on brick arches.

**7.5**: Coal carted and barged from King's Cross, 1860–1932. (RAIL 236/587 & 588, National Archives)

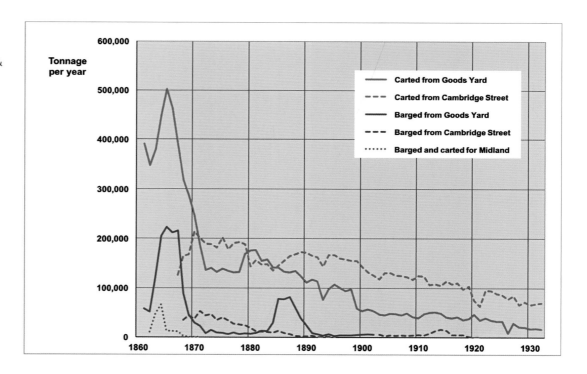

THE KING'S CROSS STORY: 200 YEARS OF HISTORY IN THE RAILWAY LANDS

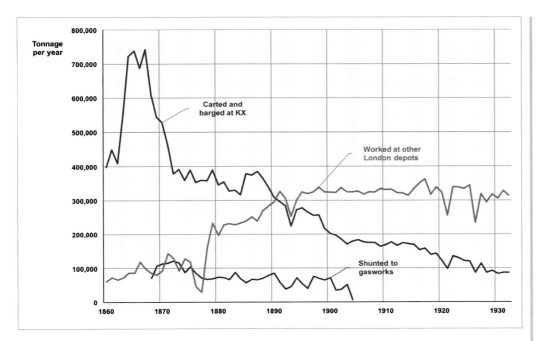

7.6: Total London coal traffic via King's Cross, 1860–1932. (RAIL 236/587 & 588, National Archives)

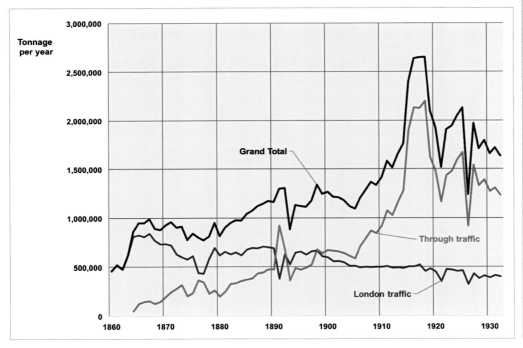

**7.7**: Total London and through coal traffic 1860–1932. (RAIL 236/587 & 588, National Archives)

# TRANSPORT FROM COALFIELD TO CONSUMER

The major sources of coal supply to the GN Company in the early years were the north-east (Durham) and South Yorkshire. It was into the latter fields that the Company extended its own rail network. The Silkstone and Elsecar Company represented the interests of South Yorkshire coal owners, including collieries at Moorend, Barnsley, Worsborough, Elsecar, Wrenthorpe and Adwalton, and established its own base with offices and stabling at King's Cross. From the early 1860s the GN was also sourcing coal from Derbyshire, where many new pits were being opened.

From the coalfield to the depot at King's Cross, coal was transported in rail wagons (7.2, page 85), usually with bottom opening doors. At the depot, if the coal was to be barged (7.3), the wagons were run to specially constructed coal drops. For coal to be delivered by road, the wagons were shunted into the various coal drops where the coal was released either into hoppers at a mezzanine level, from which the coal would fill sacks, or directly into sacks that were already on the delivery carts. A large fleet of carts was involved in the delivery of coal to the consumer (7.4).

# TONNAGES OF COAL MOVED 1860–1932

The information on coal tonnages presented in the graphs 7.5 to 7.7 (pages 86–87) is taken from *Tonnage book of the GNR Coal Depot* (RAIL 236/587), and *St Pancras, Tonnage book of Cambridge Street Coal Drop* (RAIL 236/588), both in the National Archives. The tonnages in the first source are monthly by coal merchant. The more useful second source divides the tonnages into various categories, providing data on a weekly basis.

Coal carted from the goods yard peaked dramatically at 502,000 tons in 1865 (7.5). This was followed by a steep decline over the next seven years, followed by a longer general decline, only partially compensated by a transfer of coal business to Cambridge Street, a take-up of supply by the gasworks (7.6), an increasing diversion to secondary London depots (7.6) and an increasing through traffic to other rail companies (7.7).

Some marginal notes in the archives – 'coal cheaper at waterside, ships plentiful' – may explain part of the steep fall as due to competition from the seaborne trade. The peak for carted coal from the goods yard coincided with a peak of 223,000 tons of barged coal, as the GNR captured a large part of the canal-side market, but this declined even more steeply to almost zero when the Regent's Canal Company raised their rates. Both seaborne and barged coal supplied canal-side industries dependent on large regular supplies, such as gasworks, which were price sensitive. Thus larger more reliable steam colliers were able to wrest back much of the London coal trade from rail by the 1890s.

But the main cause of decline was the Midland Railway's capture of a large share of the market and competition from the LNWR, which had taken the lead in 1861 in carrying coal to London from the many new pits opening in Derbyshire.

After 1870 the major part of the coal business transferred to Cambridge Street, which became responsible for two-thirds of the coal throughput after 1900. Most of the remaining third was gradually moved into the Coal Depot sidings (first provided in the 1860s) between the Locomotive Shed and the NLR in the north-western corner of the yard, where the unloading of coal wagons on the level avoided wastage.

After allowing for the supply of the Imperial Gas Light & Coke Company's works, the period 1870–90 was at best one of slowly declining supply from King's Cross. The GN Company faced strong competition from the Midland Company, whose coal was supplied from Derbyshire fields that were closer and therefore involved lower transport costs. Coal merchants complained to the GN Company in 1872 that the South Yorkshire coal owners:

> … demanded excessive prices and were always the initiators of an increased charge which the Derbyshire Coal owners were only too willing to follow, but that the latter never initiated progress in that direction themselves. This cause of proceeding has had its usual effect. When increased prices were asked by the South Yorkshire people the Dealers and Merchants turned to the Derbyshire, and the consequence has been a large increase in the latter trade and a serious and continued diminution in the former.

After 1890 the decline was more rapid. By 1930 only 100,000 tons per year were being handled at King's Cross. In the earlier part of this period, up to 1900, coal and other commodities were being increasingly diverted to satellite GNR depots, including Ashburton Grove, Clarence Yard, Finsbury Park, High Vale, Caledonian Road, Hackney Wick, Brick Lane and Elephant & Castle. This coincided with a rapid expansion of London into new suburbs that were more efficiently served from satellite depots than from a central depot like King's Cross. After 1900, this levelled off (7.6).

Of the three noticeable dips in supply between 1890 and 1930, the first was caused by a miners' strike from July to November 1893. The second involved a series of strikes over 1919 to 1921, first by

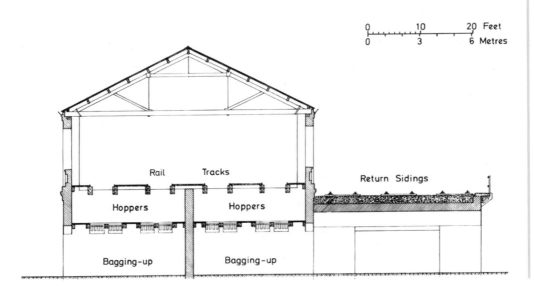

**7.8**: The Eastern Coal Drops, schematic cross-section from north, 1976. (Malcolm Tucker)

the NUR and ASLEF, and then in successive years by miners. The last dip represents the General Strike from 4–12 May 1926 and the extended miners' strike. Industrial unrest following the First World War is discussed in Chapter 10.

Even more important, in volume terms, than suburban depots was the coal business diverted to other railway companies south of the river with which the GNR had developed commercial relations. Principal among these were the London Brighton and South Coast Railway; the South Eastern and Chatham Railway; and, via Blackfriars, the London Chatham and Dover Railway. The volume of through traffic overtook London traffic in the last decade of the nineteenth century and was 75 per cent of a total of 2 million tons by the early years of the twentieth century. The Ferme Park Yard, opened between Hornsey and Haringey in 1888, became the great sorting point for through coal traffic.

This increase in through traffic resulted in a steady increase of total tonnage of coal supplied by the GNR up to the start of the First World War in 1914. From that point on, the trend line becomes rather erratic. There was a strong growth of supply during the war years, attributable to a preference for supply by rail rather than sea, which would have been more vulnerable to enemy action. After the war, the strikes of 1921 and 1926 feature strongly, as does the start of a period of economic decline in the late 1920s/early 1930s.

## COAL DROPS NORTH OF THE CANAL

**7.9**: The Eastern Coal Drops looking south, 1976. (Malcolm Tucker)

The coal drops in the goods yard comprise two long, slate-roofed ranges built by the GNR in 1850 and 1859, facing each other across a sett-paved yard.

The Eastern Coal Drops opened in 1851 to receive trains of coal wagons, which entered the building at a rail level of 88ft (26.7m) OD. Coal was discharged through bottom doors into storage hoppers located above the ground-level bays, at a road level of 70ft (21.4m) OD, where the coal was bagged up, and into which coal merchants' carts could be backed for loading. Traversers at the southern end transferred empty wagons to a flanking three-siding viaduct on the west side for return (7.8).

These triple-level, covered coal drops were themselves unusual, and distinguished by open arches on either side to let out the coal dust (7.9). They were very significant in the first rail-borne delivery of coal to London. However, Samuel Plimsoll found that the drops tended to break the soft coal that he traded and, after trials with his improved coal drops, built a new set of coal drops on the opposite bank of the Regent's Canal.

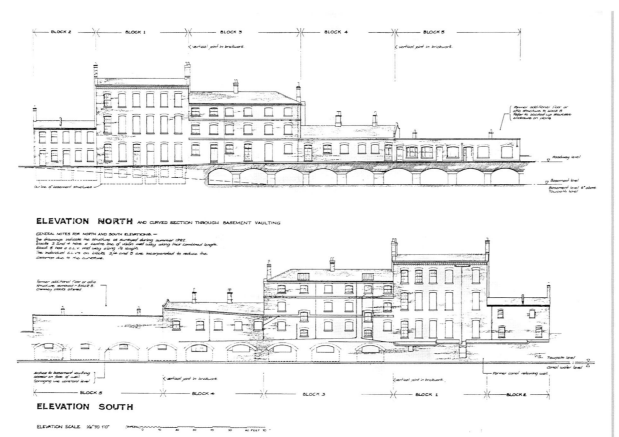

**ELEVATION NORTH** AND CURVED SECTION THROUGH BASEMENT VAULTING

GENERAL NOTES FOR NORTH AND SOUTH ELEVATIONS.—

**ELEVATION SOUTH**

ELEVATION SCALE 1/6" TO 1'0"

Above left: **7.10**: Western Coal Drops from Plimsoll Viaduct, looking north. The difference in level of the inwards and outwards lines of the viaduct can be seen, despite the tracks having been removed. (LMA)

Above right: **7.11**: The entrance to the former GNR Coal and Stone Basin below St Pancras Lock in March 1995. The windows set in the towpath retaining wall provided light to the stables under Wharf Road. (Malcolm Tucker)

Left: **7.12**: Coal and Fish Offices: North and South Elevations, an extract from a reconstructed drawing. (Michael Senatore, Industrialogical Associates)

Over the years, the Eastern Coal Drops were adapted as a goods shed and warehouses, but ten bays at the northern end remained largely unaltered until a fire in 1985.

The Western Coal Drops (7.10) opened in 1860. The three-siding timber viaduct for empty wagons, originally on the west side of the coal drops building, was rebuilt in iron, and later dismantled and re-erected on the east side of the coal drops to support a roadway when the Western Goods Shed was built in 1897–99.

The Plimsoll Viaduct was built in 1865–66 to carry coal wagons south, via a bridge – since demolished – over the canal, into the coal drops patented and owned by Sir Samuel Plimsoll. The inwards and outwards tracks of the viaduct were graded to facilitate movement of full and empty coal wagons, so there was a level difference between the two tracks (7.10).

On the east bank of the canal at the northern end of the Coal Depot, before construction of the Western Goods Shed, the Coal and Stone Basin was a two-armed open-air small dock with railway sidings alongside. To enter either basin, canal barges passed under the raised towpath and Wharf Road, upheld by a brick retaining wall. This feature was required by the general raising of ground level except in the lower yard of the Coal Depot (7.11).

On the south side of Wharf Road, to the west of Somers Bridge and the access into the goods yard, the Coal and Fish Offices were built to provide accommodation for clerical and administrative staff in several phases from 1852 to the early 1860s (7.12). But the preference of coal traders for the Cambridge Street drops created a need for coal offices on that side of the canal, at the junction of Cambridge Street with Wharf Road. The Coal and Fish Offices then assumed a variety of additional functions, housing the GNR Horse Department and Tack Room, independent hay and straw merchants and GN employees administering the fish trade.

## CAMBRIDGE STREET DEPOT

Samuel Plimsoll's first contact with the GN Board was in 1853, when he proposed supplying coal from the South Yorkshire field over the GN line. After several hiccups, including his bankruptcy, this led to a contract to supply coal via the Eastern Coal Drops. Plimsoll was not happy with the high level of breakages that were incurred when discharging from wagons to hoppers. It is likely that these breakages were due in part to the peculiar class of soft coal that he brought from South Yorkshire. He was therefore allowed, in 1860, to use one of the Company's sidings, believed to have been in Coal Drops Yard between the Eastern and Western Coal Drops, to experiment with other discharge systems. When the timber viaduct was constructed across the coal yard for access to Plimsoll's Coal Depot in Cambridge Street, part of these experimental works was demolished.

Samuel Plimsoll's coal drops in Cambridge Street started operations in July 1866 with thirteen drops. Rapid growth of business resulted in a major expansion to forty-nine drops in 1868, nine of which were extended over canal wharves to allow coal to be dropped into barges alongside.

7.13: Cambridge (now Camley) Street ('Plimsoll') Coal Drops looking south-east along the traverser, with Plimsoll bridge over Regent's Canal on left. There was space for four wagons on each of the coal drops on the right. The row of posts carries the electrical supply picked up by the traverser. (Irwell Press)

 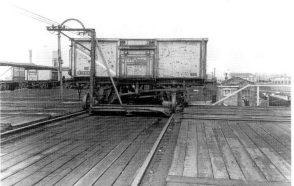

Far left: **7.14**: The view west across the coal drops towards Camley Street from the canal bridge, showing the traverser. The 'shoots' through which coal was dropped between the rails can be seen. There was a second traverser on the opposite side, alongside Camley Street. (Irwell Press)

Left: **7.15**: The view north-west across the coal drops, showing a standard 16-ton coal wagon being moved by the traverser. The electrical pick-up arrangement is clearly shown. (Irwell Press)

Further expansion of the coal drops took place after the Company purchased the lease from Plimsoll's heirs in 1891 and took over operations. By 1916 there were fifty-seven drops, each with accommodation for four wagons; the three wagons nearest the canal were used for coal in store and the end wagon nearest Cambridge Street for loading through a shoot into sacks that stood on a one-sack weighing machine. The Cambridge Street coal drops are shown in 7.13 to 7.15.

The GN charge for the services of the coal drops was 2*d* a ton in 1916, which was considered insufficient to cover the cost of services.

Gordon (1893) described the scene at Cambridge Street Depot thus:

You can see theta [*sic*] of all sorts, good, bad, and indifferent, at work in dozens up that curious thoroughfare – though it looks like a cul-de-sac – which runs out of Pancras Road under the arches by Battle Bridge, round by the gasworks and between the Midland and Great Northern Railways. There you will find coals to the left of you, coals to the right of you, volleying and thundering. In every arch is a platform; on every platform are two weighing machines; over each weighing machine is a shoot, which delivers into the sacks on the scales, and from which the coal stream is cut off with a lever much as you turn off your water at a tap. Overhead are the waggons; down the shoots the coal roars, and booms, and hisses in a cloud of dust, as sack after sack fills up and is run out on the hand truck into the vans, in the shafts of which stand the horses gently bobbing their nosebags and utterly indifferent to the dust and din.

## COAL DUTIES

Coal brought into the metropolitan area by railway was subject to coal duties levied by the Corporation of London. Coal duties were closely associated with the development of London's infrastructure and buildings. They are described in Annex 2.

# eight

# Supplying the Metropolis

## WHERE GOODS WERE HANDLED

The areas where goods were handled varied over time due to the introduction of new infrastructure, most of which was in the first fifty years of GNR operations. Goods handling in 1858 is shown in 4.1 on page 54. Some impression of the movement of goods in and out of the yard in about 1900 is given in 8.1. Plan 8.2 is from 1906, after the construction of the Western Goods Shed, the upper and lower levels of which are shown. Haslam (2016) gives a fuller picture over time.

By 1906 the decline in handling coal in the Eastern and Western Coal Drops had allowed for parts to be converted into warehouse accommodation for lease, some of which was taken up by bottle manufacturers. The Midland Goods Shed was also partially converted into bottle warehousing.

**8.1**: The York Road entrance to the goods yard, *c*.1900. (Pope/Parkhouse Archive)

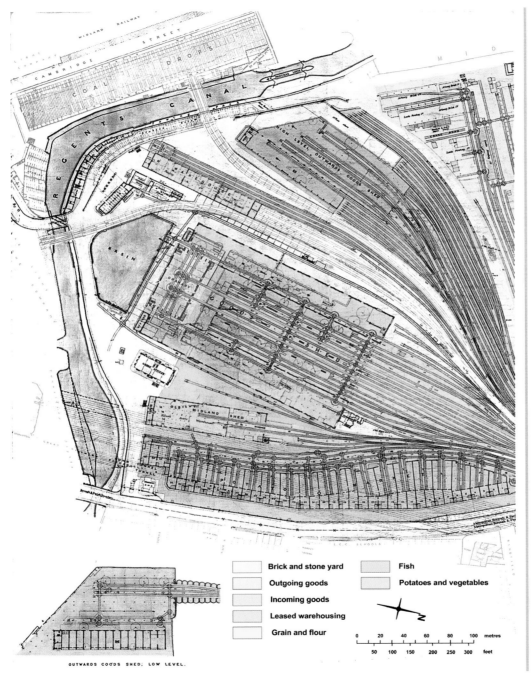

**8.2**: Incoming and outgoing commodities and warehousing of goods, an extract from the 1906 GNR plan overlaid by author. (British Railways/David Millibank Challis collections)

OUTWARDS GOODS SHED; LOW LEVEL.

| | Brick and stone yard | | Fish |
| | Outgoing goods | | Potatoes and vegetables |
| | Incoming goods | | |
| | Leased warehousing | | |
| | Grain and flour | | |

0   20   40   60   80   100   metres
50   100   150   200   250   300   feet

Inwards and outwards movement of grain and general merchandise took place in the complex of the Granary, Transit Sheds and Train Assembly Shed, up until the construction of the Western Goods Shed in 1896–97.

## STONE AND BRICK

Yorkstone was the traditional London paving stone and had been used for paving the arrival and departure platforms at King's Cross. The GNR was well placed to move this material from the quarries by rail, rather than by canal and sea to the docks. Yorkstone traffic grew rapidly, as was revealed in the mid-1850s with the demand for 100 additional stone wagons, as well as new cranes, paved roads and wharves for the Stone Dock. Limestone and sandstone for building came from a variety of quarries near the East Coast Main Line.

The last quarter of the nineteenth century was a period of intense house building in London, and brick was brought in by major companies operating in Fletton, Peterborough and elsewhere. In the 1930s, Erwood (1988) noted that immense tonnages of bricks were being hauled once again from the Fletton area for new houses being built in London and the south of England at that time.

Until the Western Goods Shed commandeered the space, stone and brick were unloaded at the northern arm of the Coal and Stone Basin and sidings alongside. Here were warehouses, offices and even stables of the stone and brick companies: Arlesey Brick and Joseph Cliff & Son of Leeds are shown on a plan of 1895 (7.1, page 83); Arlesey Brick and Leeds Fireclay Company, which took over Joseph Cliff and greatly expanded the facilities at King's Cross, on the 1906 plan (8.1).

Arlesey, on the border of Bedfordshire and Hertfordshire, had a thriving brick-making industry through to the mid-twentieth century. As of 1900 there were five brickworks around the town, known for the Arlesey White bricks produced from Gault clay.

Joseph Cliff, founder of a brickworks at Wortley near Leeds, manufactured decorative architectural stonework, sanitary ware and other enamelled products.

## THE GRANARY

The Granary was built to store grain and flour on the five floors above the ground floor, providing an area of over 80,000sq. ft (7,500m$^2$). Grain was measured by volume in a variety of units, including quarters, bushels and sacks. The Granary could store about 25,000 quarters, which was equivalent to about 5,000 tons of grain, sufficient to make some 9 million loaves of bread. A reconstruction of the Granary complex, showing the internal arrangements for movement of grain around the building, as well as movements more generally, is shown in 8.3. There was ample hydraulic power to lift sacks of grain to upper floors, and shoots that moved sacks from floor to floor and into delivery carts (8.4).

The Granary remained busy with grain and flour traffic until the First World War: thereafter grain imports and lower domestic production reduced the need for warehouse accommodation. By 1925, only two floors were needed for grain and flour, and it was decided to divert heavy Continental containerised traffic from Bishopsgate to King's Cross, adapting the three upper floors of the Granary to store the 'Continental case goods', served by an electric lift in a new lift shaft that was inserted into the north wall.

In fact, from 1926, floors two to five were given over to storing sugar for the English Sugar Beet Corporation, and from 1929 were adapted for the Corporation as a bonded warehouse.

## POTATOES, FRUIT AND VEGETABLES

The Potato Market comprised a series of warehouses leased by the big wholesale Covent Garden merchants into which were received the potatoes brought down from Lincolnshire and elsewhere, together with seasonal crops such as rhubarb and celery and other vegetables for London's millions.

The volume of potatoes handled each year varied according to the weather in the growing areas. We have data for only sixteen years between 1865 to 1939. These show that the supply to the metropolis varied from 70,000 tons per year to 120,000 tons per year, with an average of 100,000 tons. There is no obvious trend either up or down after 1870: it remained an important trade for the GNR, from which they earned about 5s (£0.25) per ton in 1877.

The narrow entrance to the Potato Market created difficulty in working the wagons delivered. Picking out the wagons required by each trader for his daily orders involved much shunting and capstan turntable work, for which there were fifty-three turntables and fourteen hydraulic capstans. The means of turning wagons into the warehouse bays using ropes and capstans can be seen in 11.3 on page 134 and the twin turntables and snatch heads outside each bay are seen in 8.5.

Storage was provided in a line of potato warehouses, built in 1864, that ran close to York Road, some with basement cellars (14.6, page 166), others with only open storage (8.5). The curved East Handyside Canopy provided roof cover from 1888 for the traffic serving the warehouses (8.5).

Once within the warehouse, the wagon could be emptied and the potatoes stacked in sacks (8.6). They were then ready for loading onto drays for distribution to customers or to other markets around London. Drays would await loading in the cart road that ran along the east side of the warehouses (8.7), just west of York Road, a roadway that was covered in 1896.

The home-grown fruit and vegetable trade was constrained, before the covering of the roof of the market, by lack of dry storage. The trade grew substantially after 1888, but data is lacking before the 1920s, when it reached about 40,000 tons per year. Such perishable produce had to reach Covent Garden in the early hours, and the hours before dawn were very busy in the Potato Market.

Trade in bananas from the West Indies grew very rapidly in the first years of the twentieth century. Imports were started about 1902 by Elders & Fyffe through Bristol and Manchester (Salford) Docks. Within three years, six more boats were in service and three were being built. It was at this point that

Elders & Fyffe, who wished to increase the service from Manchester to London, approached the GNR for heated wagons and storage accommodation in the goods yard. They were offered three bays under the new Outwards Shed, in what were formerly the Western Coal Drops.

The volume shipped via King's Cross increased from 2,255 tons in 1905 to 7,768 tons in 1907, suggesting that bananas had rapidly become a staple of many Londoners' diets.

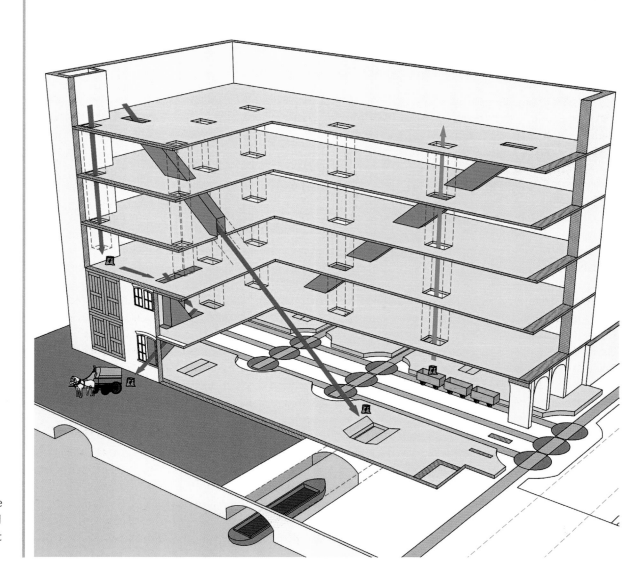

**8.3**: A cutaway showing the working of the Granary and Transit Shed. (Pre-Construct Archaeology)

THE KING'S CROSS STORY: 200 YEARS OF HISTORY IN THE RAILWAY LANDS

# MILK

Before the advent of the railways, Londoners obtained fresh milk from cows kept in the back yards or cellars of houses. In 1850 some 800,000 gallons (3.6 million litres) were brought into London by rail, 2.5 million gallons (11.4 ML) by road and 12 million gallons (55 ML) home-produced in town. By 1870 the quantities home-produced and brought in by rail were approximately equal, at about 9 million gallons (41 ML) each. By 1890 the railways were bringing in 84 per cent of the liquid milk consumed, rising to 96 per cent in 1910. Milk consumption had increased from about 6 gallons (27 litres) per head per year in 1850 to 21 gallons (95 litres) in 1910, each Londoner consuming nearly ½ pint (0.28 litres) a day. The total quantity consumed in London was therefore about 100 million gallons (455 ML) in 1910.

Milk became an important traffic for the Company in the 1880s. In 1884 King's Cross dealt with 44,273 churns (a churn held 10 gallons or 46 litres). In 1891, Henry Oakley, the General Manager, noted the rapid increase in traffic and the need for twenty milk vans to be loaded daily. He proposed that old brake vans be adapted to meet the shortfall he had identified.

The Company built special sidings at King's Cross in 1893 for the milk trade (page 47), and by 1910 about 250,000 milk churns were being delivered each year, four or five special milk trains being run every day with many other wagons attached to ordinary trains. The milk platform was formed with a low area so that trucks could be backed directly alongside rail wagons for the transfer of milk churns.

Above left: **8.4**: A reconstruction of the earliest trapdoor and chute network inside the Granary (not to scale). (Pre-Construct Archaeology)

Above right: **8.5**: The Potato Market warehouses looking north under the East Handyside Canopy, 1951. (SSPL/NRM)

**8.6**: Stacking potatoes in Warehouse 15 and hanging sacks up to dry, 1951. View to west under the 1850 departure shed roof, with 1896 Handyside roofing beyond, towards the offices and Refreshment Club at the north end of the Eastern Transit Shed. The Refreshment Club was funded both by the GNR and members' subscriptions. It provided messing facilities and social amenities to improve absenteeism and discourage staff members from frequenting pubs. (SSPL/NRM)

**8.7**: A busy scene in the cart road, fronted by potato warehouses and covered by the 1896 roof built by Andrew Handyside, with York Road on right.

## FISH

Special fish trains were a feature of the fish trade from as early as 1852, when rates of 50–80 shillings per ton were agreed with traders from Edinburgh to Sunderland for rail carriage. Herrings, either fresh, salted or smoked, were the staple of the fish trade.

As the fish trade grew, it was increasingly supplied by express goods trains run at passenger train speeds from Aberdeen, Hull and Grimsby, which had grown into the chief east coast fishing ports, arriving at King's Cross throughout the night and in the early hours.

Here, underneath the West Handyside Canopy, wagons of fish were moved onto the Long and Short Fish Roads (8.1), sidings devoted to handling fish, where they were unloaded and the fish carted to Billingsgate in the early hours. There were several warehouses and cold stores that served the Sunday morning fish market when fish was sold by auction, as Billingsgate was then closed.

## LIVESTOCK

There were no cattle or livestock sidings at King's Cross goods yard, cattle instead being taken off at sidings in the northern approaches to be driven down Market Road to the Metropolitan Cattle Market, as described in the next chapter.

There were piggeries in the area from early days, as pigs were associated with sorting waste, a business that was prevalent around Belle Isle. Piggeries were later established on a small scale on former gasworks land after it was acquired by the Company.

## BOTTLE WAREHOUSING

Kilner Bros was an internationally renowned bottle manufacturer with a very large plant in Dewsbury, well known for its rubber-sealed screw-topped preserving jars. In 1869 the GN granted Kilner Bros a twenty-one-year lease on the southern part of the Midland Goods Shed as warehouse space. In 1871 it was agreed to add a floor. Kilner also leased space in the offices in front of the Midland Goods Shed. When the Midland Goods Shed was adapted for inwards traffic during the First World War in 1915, Kilner moved to the Eastern Coal Drops.

The GN's Eastern Coal Drops, losing business to Plimsoll's Cambridge Street Coal Drops, were partly converted into warehousing for private tenants. The first block was ready in 1875 and leased to Bagley, Wild & Co. of Knottingly, Leeds, another firm of glass bottle manufacturers.

Erwood (1988), writing about his 1937 experiences, describes the Bagley operations some sixty-two years later and in the same location. The balance between humour and prejudice is not a comfortable one:

> They brought in thirty or more wagons of bottles each day, which were unloaded by their own groups of fearsome and muscular women, who were reputed in their spare moments to indulge in the sort of activity for which the King's Cross area is still noted. … Certainly I was the recipient of much outspoken comment and prurient invitation whenever I passed very hastily along the road, which ran over the end of their siding on the way to the Outwards Shed.

## GOODS HANDLING

A large proportion of the London traffic was of a light and miscellaneous character, requiring careful checking, loading and invoicing. Out of 6,860 consignments received on 5 December 1873, 4,812 (70 per cent) were less than 200lb (88kg). Those over that weight averaged 2,610lb (1,184kg). The description that follows relies on Erwood (1988).

Goods came in a great variety of packages, from 14lbs (6kg) to over 10 tons in weight. Except for the heaviest and most unwieldy items, these were manhandled in and out of box vans (4.11(c), page 61) or, less commonly, open wagons, usually of 10 or 12 tons nominal capacity, by gangs of four to six men using no equipment more sophisticated than hand barrows and cargo hooks, with occasional help from a crowbar or two.

The Goods Department's interest began once wagons had arrived at the reception sidings and the locomotive had been detached. First the labelling and documentation were checked, then the shunters took over, and, as tracks in the shed became cleared, loaded wagons were shunted up in rakes of about fifteen for unloading.

Once out of the hands of the shunters, the wagons came into the charge of the bank staff (whereas passenger stations had platforms, goods stations had 'banks'). The unloading gangs usually consisted of six men: a checker (in charge), a caller-off (the reader of address labels), and four porters who did most of the donkey work.

The easternmost bank in the Inwards Shed was marked out in spaces according to the delivery area served, and the delivery vehicles were backed up and loaded as packages were brought round by the wagon gangs. Once loaded, the van driver and his vanguard (usually a 14–15-year-old boy, and frequently the son of a railway employee) departed on their round, checking out at the Cartage Office by the main gate. On their round they would keep an eye open for cards displaying 'LNER Carman to Call'.

Returning vehicles stopped at the Cash Office by the main gate to hand over money received for goods sent 'Carriage Forward', and then, if necessary, went round to the Outwards Shed for unloading. There the bank was marked out according to the destination, and the work was more or less in the reverse order to that of the Inwards Shed. Once the outward-bound wagons were loaded and labelled, they were drawn out of the shed and marshalled for the appropriate train by the shunters, after which the Operating Department took over.

In fact, many London-bound goods trains would terminate at Ferme Park before being divided, sorted and reassembled to be sent on to King's Cross and other destinations.

## OFFICE AND PAPERWORK

Goods movements generated large quantities of paperwork and the need for armies of clerical staff. Each consignment, however small, required three documents: a consignment note, an invoice and a delivery note. Weights were entered on the consignment note and charges calculated according to a complex system, based on merchandise classification, distance and other criteria. Weights were entered in tons (1 ton equalled 2240lb), hundredweights (112lb), quarters (28lb) and pounds.

## OVERALL TONNAGES HANDLED

Data on overall tonnages handled are limited and often anecdotal. The longest run of data comes from a Goods Manager's report to the board in 1875, giving annual tonnages for 1866–74 excluding coal.

It is assumed, being from the Goods Department, that this also excludes other minerals traffic, such as stone, brick and timber. The numbers vary from 536,000 tons to 607,000 tons, with little discernible trend up or down.

A further two years' data for 1882–83 fall within the same range.

Josiah Medcalf (1900), Outdoor Goods Manager, believed the gross total of goods of all kinds, in and out, exclusive of coal, approached 1,000,000 tons. If this included the substantial traffic in stone, brick and timber, it could be consistent with the earlier tonnages.

Peter Erwood (1988) hazarded 'an educated guess that a good half million' tons of merchandise passed through King's Cross in 1937, which appears consistent with tonnages from seventy years earlier.

In summary, it could be argued that the tonnages handled over almost 100 years from the 1860s appear to have been remarkably uniform. But it only needs a glance at 6.2 on page 74 to see that the figures quoted above are inconsistent with the demand for horses. Given that cart improvements meant that horses could handle greater loads, the reality must have been a steady increase in tonnage handled, at least until the First World War – yet the limited data available do not support this.

## A CURIOUS TRADE

**8.8**: Quail catching, Northern Sinai, ILN, 8 March 1862. (Mary Evans)

The railway saw its role as supporting the growth of small as well as large enterprises, fostering the movement of goods used by any trading communities. This is an example of the special measures that the railway sometimes had to take to service particular trades.

The quail was highly regarded as a table delicacy in the UK, with demand far outstripping supply. It originates from the Great Lakes area of Central Africa, but undertakes a complex migration in spring that led vast flocks over the Sudan and up the Nile Valley before crossing the Mediterranean and heading for their summer habitats in Europe and Russia. The exhausted birds are obliged to pause before crossing the sea, and here they were netted in their thousands (8.8). They had to undergo a similar ordeal on their return journey in the autumn.

The Egyptian Quail Syndicate, headquartered in Alexandria, was the receiving house for almost all the quails caught, handling around 1 million quails each year. The birds quickly recovered after being fed and watered, and were placed in coops that accommodated 100 birds. These were loaded onto fast steamers to Manchester, and thence by train to

**8.9**: A 'quail train' at King's Cross, from a 1913 edition of *Railway Magazine*, 33. (ICE)

London, in consignments of about 100,000 quails (8.9). Experienced attendants accompanied the birds all the way to London, administering to their needs for food and water.

Arriving at King's Cross in the early hours, the birds were transferred to warehouses where they were fattened on millet, consuming about a ton a day. The cries of thousands of wild birds reached a deafening intensity, while their Egyptian attendants glided from coop to coop.

# nine

# Belle Isle and Northern Approaches

## NORTHERN APPROACHES

The northern approaches to the Railway Lands lie outside the area with which we are primarily concerned, but they exerted a strong influence on its development. The features described are shown in 9.1.

## NORTH LONDON RAILWAY

The North London Railway was built at the same time as the GNR and formed the northern boundary of the Railway Lands. It offered the GNR an important route to the London Docks and the GNR made connections to the NLR as early as 1853.

The engraving (9.2) shows the Camden Town Viaduct of the NLR where it crosses the GNR in a girder bridge. Beyond the NLR Viaduct, the southern portal of Copenhagen Tunnel can be seen.

In the foreground, the up passenger train on the left is about to arrive at the Maiden Lane Temporary Passenger Station and is passing signal box 'C' on Captain Galton's plan of signals (2.9, page 31). The small house with a pier extending over the embankment must be for the signalman. There appears to be a ticket collection platform on the east side of this line. A goods train laden with spoil from construction is shown heading north on the branch leading from Gasworks Tunnel and the main passenger station. Given the spoil removal method adopted by John Jay, this appears to be artistic licence, as does the three-track branch given that only two tracks were laid, as shown by Galton. Other features must also be challenged, notably the unsupported span on the west side of the NLR Viaduct, which was in fact on embankment.

Several features can be distinguished in the background, accepting some artistic licence in their positioning. From left to right we can observe Adams' tile kilns at Belle Isle; St Paul's Church, Camden Square; Highgate Church; Copenhagen House, still approachable from the south over open Copenhagen Fields; and Pentonville Model Prison.

A contract for widening the NLR, quadrupling the tracks between Camden and Dalston, was let in February 1868. All the widening was done on the north side. The most significant works, other than stations, were the widening of Camden Viaduct and the NLR Viaduct over the GNR.

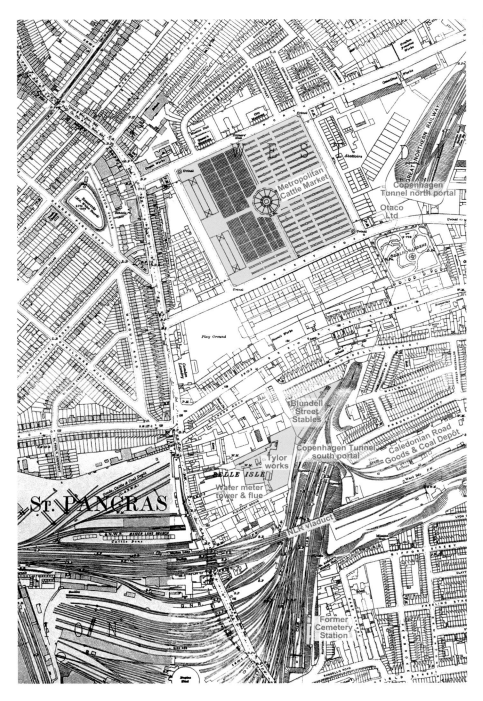

**9.1**: A general plan of the northern approaches overlaid by author. (OS, edition 1913–14)

**9.3**: Major Courtney (Cecil Parker) and Louis Harvey (Herbert Lom) on the roof of Mrs Wilberforce's house, *The Ladykillers*, 1955. (Mary Evans)

The NLR Viaduct is seen from the north in a still from *The Ladykillers* (9.3) whilst they are on the roof of Mrs Wilberforce's house, overlooking the mainline at the south portal of the Copenhagen Tunnel. A steam train is heading north while a goods train is crossing on the NLR Viaduct. Louis Harvey (Herbert Lom) is the hitman confronting Major Courtney (Cecil Parker).

## BELLE ISLE

Belle Isle had long been notorious for its noxious industry, even before the arrival of the railway, as noted in Chapter 1. A letter in *The Times* in 1855 described the 'pestilential miasma' from the factories.

The cattle market must have influenced the industry already attracted to the area by the canal and railway. Unsavoury businesses, from tripe factories to horse slaughterers, established themselves in the area, alongside breweries, tile kilns and chemical industries, adding to the gasworks (gas, tar, coke processing), coal depots and open sewers. Belle Isle was graphically described by James Greenwood, a social explorer, journalist and writer, in his 1874 book *In Strange Company*:

But you do not arrive at Belle-Isle proper until you reach the archway that spans the road. At this point you may dispense with the services of your faithful olfactory guide; indeed, it will be better, provided you do it in a way that shall not be remarkable – for the act is one that the inhabitants may resent – to mask its

**9.4**: Outside the Fortune of War public house at 184 York Road, in the early 1880s. Next door at No. 186, the engraved wall panel heralds 'John Atcheler, Horse Slaughterer to Her Majesty'. (Historic England)

keen discrimination with your pocket handkerchief. Here, an appropriate sentinel at the threshold of this delectable place, stands the great horse-slaughtering establishment of the late celebrated Mr. John Atcheler.

As a horse-slaughtering establishment nothing can be said against it. I am afraid to say how many hundred lame, diseased, and worn-out animals weekly find surcease of sorrow within Atcheler's gates – or how many tons of nutriment for the feline species are daily boiled in the immense coppers and carried away every morning by a legion of industrious barrowmen. Everything, I have no doubt, is managed in the best possible way; but that best still leaves a terribly broad margin for odours that can only be described as nauseating. In the shadow of the slaughter-yard is a public-house – a house of call for the poleaxe men and those who, with a hook to catch fast hold, and an enormous knife, denude the worn-out horses' bones of the little flesh that remains attached to them.

They are terrible looking fellows, these honest horse slaughterers. They seem rather to cultivate than avoid stains of a crimson colour; and they may be seen at the bar of the public-house before-mentioned, merry as sandboys, haw-hawing in the true and original 'fee-fo-fum' tone, drinking pots of beer with red hands and with faces that look as though they had been swept with a sanguinary hearth-broom. You can see all this from the gateway where the savage young Belle-Islanders congregate to give fierce prods with pointed sticks at the miserable bare-ribbed old horses as they come hobbling in.

The spot that holds the horse slaughter houses is modestly called 'The Vale'; the first turning beyond is, with goblin like humour, designated 'Pleasant Grove'. It is hardly too much to say, that almost every trade banished from the haunts of men, on account of the villanous smells and the dangerous atmosphere which it engenders is represented in Pleasant Grove. There are bone boilers, fat-melters, 'chemical works', firework makers, lucifer-match factories, and several most extensive and flourishing dust-yards, where – at this delightful season so excellent for ripening corn – scores of women and young girls find employment in sifting the refuse of dust-bins, standing knee-high in what they sift.

Beyond the delectable Pleasant Grove is another thoroughfare called Brandon Road. Brandon Road has cottages on either side of the way, and gives harbourage to several hundred cottagers little and big. The road is hemmed in, as Pleasant Grove is, by stench-factories, and the effect on an individual used to ordinarily wholesome air is simply indescribable.

Here, in Belle-Isle, and in a few other places that might be mentioned, we have hundreds of poor, patient little boys and girls, who never in their lives did a dishonest thing, kept in ignorance and doomed to work through their young lives in dirt and squalor and the very shadow of death, for little if anything more in the shape of wages than the free street Arab contrives to pick up in his vagabond rovings.

John Atcheler's premises were sold to Harrison Barber who had six other depots in London and acquired a virtual monopoly.

## METROPOLITAN CATTLE MARKET

The removal of Smithfield Market from the city out to a suburb was long overdue, but it was opposed by the Corporation of London, who were supported by many vested interests. It came about after the

**9.5**: A busy market day at the Metropolitan Cattle Market in Copenhagen Fields, Islington, in 1856. (LMA, the Sir Charles Wakefield Collection)

purchase by the Corporation of Copenhagen House and 75 acres of Copenhagen Fields, bounded on one side by Maiden Lane.

The Corporation of London demolished the house and built the Metropolitan Cattle Market on 30 acres (12ha), opened by Prince Albert on 13 July 1855. In the centre, surrounded by pens, was a 150ft (46m) clock tower with market bells and an illuminated clock. Its base held banks, telegraph offices and the market superintendent's offices (9.5). A drovers' lodgings, five public houses and two hotels were put up around the market, and the Corporation built a block of working-class dwellings.

A new road, Market Road, was to run from Maiden Lane to Caledonian Road. It was connected by rail to the NLR and thence to the GNR, the Midland and GWR, linking with the main areas of livestock supply.

The market formed an 800ft (244m) square, paved with granite and surrounded by handsome red railings. Surrounding the square were various supporting services: lairs, slaughter-houses, tripe-dressers, cat's meat boilers, cat's gut spinners, bone boilers, glue makers and tallow smelters. There were public houses at each of the four corners: the Lamb, the White Horse, the Golden Lion and the Black Bull.

The market held 6,600 bullocks and 36,000 sheep, and the lairs held 3,000 cattle and 10,000 sheep. It was said to be the largest cattle market in the world.

An interview with Billy Osborne in *King's Cross Voices*, recorded by Alan Dein in about 2005, brings the scenes around the cattle market before the Second World War to life:

If you played off [truanted] from school you could get a shilling a load for helping the drovers drive the cattle up into the pens. For years, I couldn't work out why the cattle got out – they went mad and had to be shot – when they got round the corner to Market Road or North Road – they could smell the blood in the abattoir. They didn't drive them straight in but into pens that are now where the Astroturf is on Market Road. Next-door used to be the tripe factory. They used to boil it and the stench was unbelievable and that's why I've never liked tripe. All the old 'uns in my family liked it – it was a staple dish then – my Nan used to cook it in onions and milk. The factory was in Market Road. The fascia is still there opposite the little gardens. There was a smell of that at that end. Then in York Way there was a little boozer called The Fortune of War and next to that the knacker's yard, where they used to knock over all the horses from the railway. They boiled down all the hooves for glue – the horse-meat was cooked there – we had a horse-meat lady come round with the docks with a basket and you'd have two penneth of whatever.

You talk about the smells of the area – Market Road and the slaughterhouse and knacker's yard.

Also the steam trains. That pervaded the whole area – the smell of smoke and steam – even up to the Square. The trains used to pull out of King's Cross and come to the end of Agar Grove – all the kids were into train numbers and we'd sit on that cutting. Now they have fences as high as – we never dreamt of throwing anything over the top. We used to sit up there quite happy all day long taking numbers. You'd get smothered in smoke and steam and covered in cinders. It IS the smell of King's Cross you recall. Most predominantly coal and steam and smoke. Up York Way you could smell the processing of the stuff coming out of the abattoir and the knacker's yard.

The other thing – talking about horses – the smell of horse dung. There was such a rich mixture. Then we had the smogs. It really came down bad – most of the industries around there were producing it.

How bad was the smog there?

Oh – a pea-souper! I can remember in the early sixties, walking up York Way just by Copenhagen Street and I couldn't see the other side of the road.

## GREAT NORTHERN CEMETERY STATION

The Great Northern London Cemetery Company was constituted in 1855 to establish a burial ground at Colney Hatch, now better known as New Southgate. The 150 acres (59ha) acquired by the Colney Hatch Company, as it was referred to at the time, were about 7 miles (11km) north of King's Cross and intended to provide access to new out-of-town cemeteries for the poorer classes, for whom the cost of funeral arrangements had been unaffordable.

Under the agreement with the cemetery company, the GNR provided two stations, one at Maiden Lane, almost opposite the Belle Isle signal box, and the other at New Southgate. Special trains for coffins and mourners were run between the two stations from 1861, initially about twice a week.

The large two-storey building erected at Maiden Lane (9.6) was part mortuary, part railway station. There were facilities for entering at street level, a lift to lower the coffin to a vault at platform level, where the body could be preserved until the funeral, and waiting rooms for mourners that wished to pay their respects.

The cemetery company ceased regular operations in 1863 and, following a brief resumption of special trains to cope with the massive cholera outbreak in the East End in 1864, ceased completely in 1865, selling their premises at King's Cross and Colney Hatch to the GNR in 1876. For many years the Cemetery Station was a GNR/LNER clothing store, and the blackened imposing shape of the Cemetery Station remained until 1962, when it was replaced by a concrete works.

9.6: King's Cross Cemetery Station in 1954. (ILHC)

## COPENHAGEN TUNNEL

So named from its passing under Copenhagen Fields, the first brick for Copenhagen Tunnel was laid on 27 March 1849, and the tunnel completed over the next two years. It is 594 yards (543m) long.

The current middle bore is the original tunnel and from 1886 took down trains both fast and slow.

The western bore was built in 1877 for Up and Down Goods lines at a somewhat higher level, to enable goods trains coming from the north to cross over the passenger lines at the north end of the existing tunnel, and so get a clear run into the goods yard, without interfering with the passenger traffic.

The eastern bore was built in 1886 taking up trains, both fast and slow. The area above the tunnel was used for a rail line going to the Caledonian Road Coal and Goods Depot, which opened in March 1878.

The southern portal of Copenhagen Tunnel was made famous in scenes from *The Ladykillers* when members of the gang were wheeled by barrow to be tipped into passing wagons (9.7).

The ascent from Gasworks Tunnel, under the five arches of the Maiden Lane Viaduct, under the NLR, through Copenhagen Tunnel and up Holloway Bank, was always an effort for steam locomotives, as may be seen in both 9.7 and 9.8.

The tripe factory on Market Road that is described in the extract from *King's Cross Voices* was purchased in the 1950s by Otto Fischel, a Czech refugee, who turned it into Otaco Ltd, a factory that produced plastic injection mouldings. The factory became the base for his wife Käthe Strenitz and her drawing and painting excursions into the surrounding areas as well as further afield. Two of her drawings of the northern approaches are shown on page 115 (9.9 and 9.10). Others are in Chapters 11 and 13.

**9.7**: The first gang member en route to his fate: the Professor (Alec Guinness) and One-Round Lawson (Danny Green) disposing of Major Courtney into a passing goods train, *The Ladykillers*, 1955. They have just crossed the track over Copenhagen Tunnel leading to Caledonian Goods and Coal Depot. (Mary Evans)

**9.8**: Gresley 'A4' Pacific No. 60017 *Silver Fox* blasts out of Copenhagen Tunnel on the climb away from King's Cross on 11 July 1953 with the northbound Elizabethan express for Edinburgh Waverley. (Brian Morrison)

# CALEDONIAN MARKET

Bartholomew Fair at Smithfield had achieved international importance by the seventeenth century and featured sideshows, prizefighters, musicians, wire-walkers, acrobats, puppets, freaks and wild animals. A trading event for cloth and other goods as well as a pleasure fair, the event drew crowds from all classes of society.

The fair was suppressed in 1855 by the City authorities for encouraging debauchery and public disorder. It gradually moved to the Metropolitan Cattle Market, which had just been established. Soon the Cockney costermongers, who had traded beside the old Smithfield Market, came to the new market to claim a 'pitch on the stones' (Brown, 1946).

The Metropolitan Cattle Market thus accommodated the Caledonian Market, the largest flea market in London. At the turn of the century, antiques suddenly became the vogue, so market folk turned the 'Cally' into an antique centre. Its reputation and stories of fabulous bargains drew tourists from all over the world and attracted the celebrities of the day: Walter Sickert was a habitué. The market also drew social documentary photographers like Bill Brandt and Edith Tudor-Hart. It was a rakish and irresistible hotchpotch of noise, romance, glamour, rags and riches expanding into bric-a-brac and antiques (9.11).

Held in the setting of the cattle pens, Caledonian Market operated on Tuesdays and Fridays from the 1870s until 1939. The gates opened at 10.00 a.m. with a wild rush for a good pitch. On a fine day there were up to 2,500 traders. There was nothing you could not buy in the market, animate or inanimate. A large part was devoted to fruit and vegetables.

It ceased trading during the war and was refused permission to reopen after the war due to rationing.

Above left: **9.9**: The north portal of Copenhagen Tunnel with Otaco Ltd factory on Market Road and Caledonian Market Clock Tower. Käthe Strenitz, pen and wash, late 1960s, courtesy of Käthe Strenitz Estate. (LMA)

Above right: **9.10**: The view from the north end of Copenhagen Tunnel, showing the skew bridge and the railway tracks after they were electrified. Käthe Strenitz, pen and wash, c. 1978, courtesy of Käthe Strenitz Estate. (LMA)

# GOODS AND MINERAL JUNCTION

As Charlie Mayo (2012) observed:

> There is something really beautiful about King's Cross early on a fine autumn morning. The sun in a gentle haze, delicately picks out the rails and they shine in endless ribbons, crossing and intercrossing at the points, so that they look like gossamer in a spider's web with the sun shining through it.

All the goods and locomotive sidings debouched on to the main line just south of Goods and Mineral Junction, where the view of the goods yard 'throat' taken from the NLR Viaduct is shown in 9.12. The Goods and Mineral signal box is prominent in the foreground, while arches A to E, and the narrower Arches 1 to 11, of the York Way Viaduct are visible in the background. The Up and Down Engine lines to the Top Shed locomotive depot, by now removed, had passed through Arches 1 and 2. The vacated track bed of the Caledonian Road Goods and Coal Depot Line Viaduct passes behind the signal box. The complex structure of the Caledonian Viaduct and signal box support is evident where the North London Incline line passed below, the track bed being sufficiently wide for its earlier double tracks. To the far left lie Gasworks Tunnel and the passenger lines, with the Down South London Goods line rising to their right.

**9.11**: 'For the price you like' – treasure-seeking at Caledonian Market 'on the Stones'. Note the pub in the background, one of four similar pubs on each corner of the market, *Christian Herald*, 27 November 1912. (LMA)

# CALEDONIAN GOODS AND COAL DEPOT

In 1878, major remodelling works were undertaken, costing almost £200,000, that involved King's Cross Station yard, York Road Station and signalling works up to a new box at Belle Isle. The Caledonian Road Coal Depot was the most costly element of these works, access from King's Cross goods yard requiring a long and steep viaduct passing behind Goods & Mineral signal box and under the NLR Bridge to a reversing siding beyond the south portals of Copenhagen Tunnel. This led back over the portal to Caledonian Road Goods and Coal Depot (see 6.10 and 9.7).

By the mid-1930s, many of the coal sidings in the goods yard had been moved to Caledonian Road. The Goods and Coal Depot closed in 1967.

# EBONITE TOWER

The Ebonite Tower was a familiar landmark until it was demolished in June 1983. It was so conspicuous that Luftwaffe maps had identified it (at that time called the Tylor Tower) as an aid for bombing the nearby goods yard, as was discovered after the Second World War.

The tower was renamed by the plastics manufacturer that took over the works from the founders and used it as a boiler flue for the factory. It had originally had a far more sophisticated purpose. J. Tylor & Sons Limited, established in 1787, was the first firm to produce water-metering devices on a large scale. They established the Tylor factory at Belle Isle on a site that had formerly been tile kilns, acquired from Adams in 1870. To test and calibrate their meters, they needed large quantities of water at known and constant pressure. This was achieved by setting three water tanks at different heights in a water tower some 150ft (46m) high. A large flue passed through an aperture in the three tanks, providing a draught for the boilers and ensuring the tanks did not freeze in winter.

The location of the Tylor works is shown in 9.1, and the factory layout with the pressure-testing tower is shown in 9.13. The railway tracks of one of the GNR lines linking with the goods yard can be seen immediately beyond the factory shed.

Tylor's technology distinguished it from that of the firm's noxious neighbours at Belle Isle.

## COPENHAGEN FIELDS MODEL RAILWAY

Moving forward in time, the Model Railway Club, the oldest model railway society in the world, has been developing the Copenhagen Fields Model Railway since the early 1980s. It is a detailed recreation of the northern approaches to King's Cross, set roughly between the wars – although the stock on it ranges from the 1900s up to the Second World War. Additional detail is currently being added at the southern end, which extends into part of the King's Cross goods depot.

The track and rolling stock are all made to 2mm fine scale standards, a scale of 1:152, while the track gauge is 9.42mm. This is like N gauge, except that the wheels and track are much finer, and nearly everything is handmade. The model measures 9m by 3m in area but gives a larger impression because a diminishing scale is used in the background, the model scale reducing to 1:450 at the back scene.

The street on the left in 9.14, forming the eastern boundary of the model, is Caledonian Road, complete with trams, buses, trucks, cars and horse-drawn carts. In the middle ground the railway emerges from the northern portal of Copenhagen Tunnel, the well-tended allotments of Holloway Bank lining the cutting on both sides. A goods train is crossing from east to west to deliver coal to the King's Cross Depot, while a double-headed passenger train is bound for Edinburgh. In the middle distance, the clock tower of the cattle market dominates the surrounding space. The Ebonite Tower is seen in the distance. The scale and extent of the model are apparent.

The view in 9.15 shows the Caledonian Goods and Coal Depot in the left foreground and the North London Railway crossing the approaches to the southern portal of Copenhagen Tunnel. Two trains are approaching Copenhagen Tunnel: the nearer is a passenger express headed by an A4 locomotive (*Dominion of Canada*) on its way to Scotland, while the further one has left the goods station, emerging from the fan of lines that pass under York Way Viaduct. A goods train is crossing the NLR Bridge and Viaduct, the NLR having been widened to four tracks in 1871. The Ebonite Tower and works are prominent.

**9.12**: The Goods and Mineral signal box, looking south from the NLR Bridge in the early morning of March/April 1970. (Stephen Gwinnett)

**9.13**: Tylor's water meter manufacture and testing works. (ILHC)

**9.14**: Copenhagen Fields Model Railway, looking south from Market Road. The view is from the intersection of Caledonian Road and North Road, Tony Wright. (MRC)

**9.15**: Copenhagen Fields Model Railway, looking west over Caledonian Goods and Coal Depot, Tony Wright. (MRC)

# ten

# LNER Years

## REORGANISATION FOLLOWING GROUPING

The London & North Eastern Railway (LNER) was created under the provisions of the Railways Act, which received royal assent on 19 August 1921. The LNER was the second largest of the groups that came into existence that day. It was to be formed from the constituent companies: Great Northern; Great Central; Great Eastern; North Eastern; Hull & Barnsley; North British; and Great North of Scotland, together with almost thirty subsidiary companies. The constituent companies of the grouping were given until 1 January 1923 to present an agreed scheme of amalgamation.

The 1921 Act required the complete amalgamation of these companies and the merging of their assets in a new capital structure. Close ties had already been formed by the railway companies that cooperated in passenger and freight services in the new LNER domain, but the railway companies still had a strong sense of their individual identities, as well as responsibility to their shareholders. Pooling these companies into an effective organisation to meet the needs of the new and larger corporation was even harder than pooling the rolling stock.

The close association that departmental officers from the different companies had enjoyed on the East Coast Route from London to Aberdeen had created a common purpose that helped the founding of the new company. This received further emphasis with the election of an experienced Scottish railwayman as Chairman, William Whitelaw. The Chairman and his Chief General Manager, Ralph Wedgwood, were to provide continuity of leadership, guiding the LNER for the next eighteen years until William Whitelaw announced his resignation in the autumn of 1938. Sir Ralph Wedgwood retired six months later, only to be swiftly nominated by the Ministry of Transport as Chairman of the Railway Executive Committee, which, behind the scenes, was preparing plans for running the railways in the event of war.

The Chief General Manager headed an organisation with three geographical divisions: the Scottish, the North Eastern, and the Southern, each led by a Divisional General Manager. The Group Headquarters and that of the Chief General Manager were in London at King's Cross.

The financial position of the railways after the First World War was very different from that before. The government, through the Railways Executive Committee, had brought all the railways together under one authority on 5 August 1914. It set wages, fares and levels of compensation, paying rental equivalent to net revenue earned in 1913, although the value of money had halved in the intervening period (Annex 1). In 1917, without consulting railway managers, the government had committed them to the introduction of an eight-hour day as soon as the war was over.

William Whitelaw calculated that in 1923, by comparison with 1913, there had been an increase of 148 per cent in the railways wages bill. The cost of coal had risen by 80–90 per cent, but freight and passenger rates had to be reduced to 50–60 per cent above pre-war rates to counter the falling off in trade. Large arrears of upkeep of equipment had still to be undertaken.

Such was the hard world into which the LNER was launched.

## WHY WAS THE LNER SO POOR?

None of the four grouped railway companies were as dependent on goods traffic as the LNER. No less than two-thirds of the company's annual turnover came from freight, leaving just one-third of its turnover from passengers, despite its heavily used commuter services.

Of the various forms of freight traffic, by far the most important in terms of tonnage was that of coal, both for the home market and for export. In 1923, the first year of grouping, total output from all of Britain's coalfields amounted to 273 million tons, more than a third for export. Of this, the LNER carried 102 million tons (10.1). Yet Britain had reached peak coal production in 1913–14 and coal production had been declining ever since. The LNER's coal receipts dropped from £14.7 million in 1923 to £7.9 million in 1926.

The LNER served a large part of the country where agriculture was the mainstay of the economy. The decline of agriculture in the 1920s and 1930s further weakened the Company.

The legal position of all railways in Britain was that of a common carrier, meaning that railways were compelled, with few exceptions, to accept all traffic offered, whatever its nature or potential profitability. These conditions were never imposed on the road transport industry as it grew rapidly after the First World War, and this was a perennial grievance with the railway companies. They also faced regulation from the Railway Rates Tribunal, which dictated how much they could charge for their traditional traffic.

Another handicap was the obligation to accept private owner wagons, often built to a lower specification, incompatible with efficient working, all of which had to be returned to their owners' premises when empty.

Firms packing their goods in boxes and crates charged their customers a substantial deposit against their return, and consequently the railways were forced to accept these empties to carry at unprofitable rates back to their owners. Four Arch, the area between the Locomotive Depot and the NLR, was used for this highly unprofitable business to avoid it accumulating elsewhere in the goods yard.

Net revenue, £14 million in 1923, the first year of grouping, fluctuated on a downward trend until the end of the interwar period. It not only failed to recover, but reached a new low of £6.7 million in 1938, with a drastic loss of traffic to roads, before the Wedgwood inspired Square Deal Campaign introduced greater road regulation and promoted a rail recovery in 1939.

## POST-WAR DEVELOPMENTS

The need for additional passenger platforms at King's Cross had become urgent. At grouping, there were two main departure platforms, separated by four coach sidings; four main arrival platforms, one that could accommodate two shorter trains; three suburban platforms; and the up and down platforms serving Moorgate trains, the former at York Road, the latter on Hotel Curve. This made an effective total of twelve platforms.

In 1922, the station locomotive yard was re-sited from the north-west corner of King's Cross Station, next to the Suburban Station, to the former gasworks basin, south of Goods Way and immediately west of the approach to Gasworks Tunnel (10.2). A 70ft turntable by Ransome & Rapier was installed there in 1924.

This allowed two new suburban platforms to be added to the three already existing platforms. The four carriage sidings on the main departure side were replaced by a full-length island platform while, on the arrival side, the two shorter platforms became one longer one. The station now had fifteen full-length platforms.

## INDUSTRIAL UNREST

The period following the First World War was characterised by industrial unrest, with a series of railway and colliery strikes over 1919–21, referred to in Chapter 7 in terms of their impact on coal traffic. Cumulatively these had dire consequences for rail freight

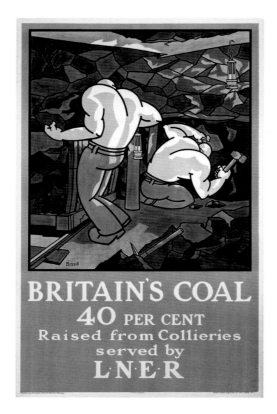

**BRITAIN'S COAL**
**40 PER CENT**
**Raised from Collieries**
**served by**
**L·N·E·R**

**10.1**: An LNER poster promotion of its dependence on coal, used from 1923, George Bisil. (SSPL/NRM)

**10.2**: The construction of Passenger Locomotive Depot from the former gasworks canal basin, 1922. (Robin Gell)

as exports of coal fell, imports rose, and customers became increasingly aware of road transport as a commercial option.

The importance of coal traffic to the LNER became only too clear when the miners went on a prolonged strike in 1926 from May to September which, from 4–12 May, was accompanied by the General Strike. The loss of coal traffic during the strike was bad enough, but what hit the LNER more than any other railway was that a very large proportion of the export traffic was lost forever, despite desperate efforts to encourage traffic after the strike.

A far less momentous consequence of the strike is shown in 10.3, with the accumulation of milk churns on Platform 1 at King's Cross.

The Company responded to the General Strike by running trains with managerial staff, men who remained at work, and volunteers, with increasing success over the nine days of the strike. Women volunteers tended to deal with the horses, although not in the case of the Hospital Stables at King's Cross during the 1919 railway strike by the NUR and ASLEF (10.4).

**10.3**: Milk churns accumulating on Platform 1 on the fourth day of the General Strike, May 1926.

While an important act of solidarity, the timing of the General Strike was unfortunate for railwaymen as the Company, motivated by what it considered supreme disloyalty, took advantage of the situation. Following the strike, the Chief General Manager issued a notice to staff (10.5) that set out some of the measures the Company adopted to reduce its workforce.

Wedgwood further directed:

- The greatest care should be taken to ensure that only the minimum number of men required to deal with the traffic is taken on.
- Shopmen: only 50 per cent of the staff in each grade to be taken back.
- It is assumed that the dispute in the coal trade is continued for the present, and no staff solely engaged in connection with the mineral traffic must be re-engaged.

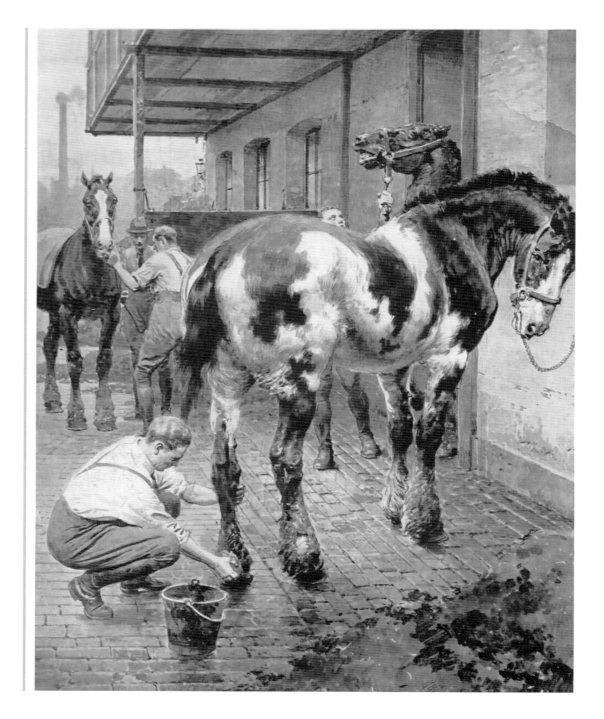

**10.4**: Volunteers attending to sick horses in the Hospital Stables during a railway strike, October 1919, Fortunino Matania, *The Sphere*. (Museum of London)

# FLYING SCOTSMAN AND SERVICE TO THE NORTH

In 1888, driven by commercial rivalry, the East Coast and West Coast consortia started competing fiercely over the speed of their express services on these two routes. In 1895, a second 'race' broke out, but this time with the added excitement of arriving at the same station in Aberdeen. Indeed, after some 500 miles from London, the two routes converged to being in sight of each other just before Kinnaber Junction, from where there was a single track to Aberdeen.

To achieve the high speeds, very few carriages could be pulled and so a second, longer, slower train had to follow on behind. There was no benefit to the public in arriving so very early and, apart from the publicity, it made no financial sense.

In a leading article *The Engineer* magazine concluded:

> One gratifying result of the race will be perhaps to silence the boasting of the American press. The far-famed Empire State Express has been thoroughly beaten.

After a fatal derailment at speed on the WCML, an agreement was reached to reassure the public and slow the runs from London to Edinburgh and Glasgow; they would now take a minimum time of eight hours. This agreement lasted into the early 1930s, removing any impetus towards improving express train performance or scheduling, which became badly outdated as a result.

In 1927 LNER started the famous non-stop express Flying Scotsman service from London to Edinburgh. The old agreement was respected and speeds kept low, but time was gained from 1928 by making the run non-stop over the whole distance of 393 miles (632km), the longest non-stop run anywhere in the world, which attracted worldwide attention (10.6). This was done through the introduction by Nigel Gresley of corridor tenders (5.13, page 70), which allowed engine crew changes at speed, the only examples of their kind. Nevertheless, the train kept to the same eight and a half hour schedule, so the average speed was just 47mph, the same as a later stopping train. It was not until 1932, no less than thirty-seven years after the race to Aberdeen, that the East Coast route was accelerated.

To add to the attraction, new trains were introduced that included a cocktail bar, hairdressing compartment and retiring room for ladies, sophistication that was celebrated by railway posters (10.7 and 10.8). But behind the glamour of the world's longest non-stop run lay the inescapable fact that the LNER was, by a considerable margin, the most impoverished of the big four, only able to invest very slowly in upgrading its suburban and goods services.

## HIGH POINT OF STEAM

Nigel Gresley (10.9) was Chief Mechanical Engineer from 1911–41 and the foremost locomotive designer. He reached the pinnacle of his career in his later years, from 1934, which have been recognised as the greatest years of LNER locomotive history. Gresley (1876–1941) was knighted in 1936 and elected President of the Institution of Mechanical Engineers, as well as receiving an honorary

# LONDON & NORTH EASTERN RAILWAY

# STRIKE OF RAILWAYMEN

The London and North Eastern Railway Company regret to announce that they have been unable to arrange with large numbers of their Staff for the resumption of duty to-day. The Staff who are still on strike have been informed that they will be re-engaged as and when there is work available for them, but this is subject to two conditions:

    1. Every Railwayman who left his work without proper notice has committed a breach of contract and has thereby involved the Railway Company in heavy losses. The Railway Company are notifying all the men who offer themselves for re-employment that the Company reserve any rights they possess to damages for breach of contract.

    2. A number of the Company's staff occupying positions of responsibility in which they were entrusted with the supervision of other members of the Staff have gone on strike. The Company propose to examine these cases individually, and to decide in each case whether they can re-employ the man concerned in the position which he occupied before the Strike. Pending this consideration they are not prepared to re-employ the men concerned who, in addition to their breach of contract, have been guilty of a breach of trust towards the Railway Company.

The Company are of the opinion that their action on these two points is essential if the future is to be free from the unwarranted disturbances which have too often occurred in connection with Railway working in the past, and they trust that the public will support them in insisting upon these safeguards for future peace and discipline in the Railway world.

R. L. WEDGWOOD

King's Cross Station, N.1            *Chief General Manager.*
13th May, 1926.

**10.5**: A warning to striking railwaymen from the Chief General Manager at the end of the General Strike, 13 May 1926. (National Archives)

**10.6**: The departure of the *Flying Scotsman* on its first non-stop King's Cross–Edinburgh run, 1 May 1928.

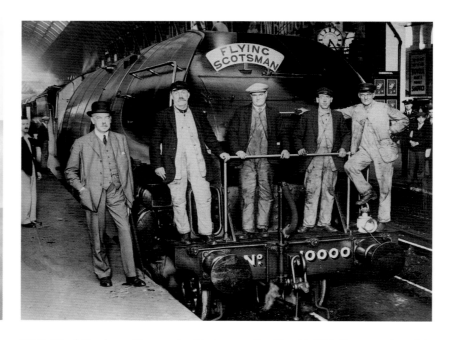

**10.9**: Nigel Gresley with crew beside locomotive No. 10,000, the experimental high-pressure compound steam locomotive, at King's Cross Station in 1930. Known as the 'Hush-Hush', the 10,000 was one of the locomotives used on the Flying Scotsman service. It proved costly to maintain and failed to achieve the hoped-for fuel economies. (SSPL/NRM)

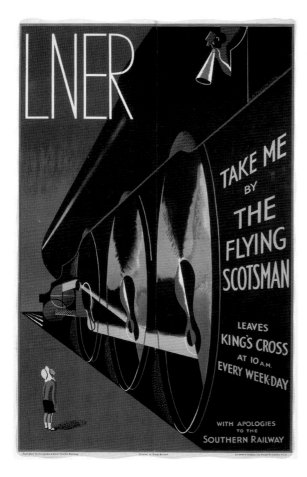

doctorate from Manchester University. His statue was erected in 2016 in the new departures concourse at King's Cross Station (16.5, page 190).

In 1933 the German streamlined diesel-electric *Flying Hamburger,* travelling the 286km between Berlin and Hamburg in 138 minutes, laid down a challenge for high-speed passenger work that Gresley took up. He believed that he could improve on the diesel performance with steam power and British coal, and he proved this with some convincing trial runs, first between King's Cross and Leeds, then King's Cross and Newcastle. Gresley, supported by the Chief General Manager, was given the approval of the LNER Board to go ahead with further development.

This saw the emergence in September 1935 of No. 2509 *Silver Link* (10.10), pioneer of the streamlined A4 Pacific class, built at the Doncaster works. In honour of the silver jubilee of King George V, the new King's Cross–Newcastle express was to be called the *Silver Jubilee,* and the carriages and four

**10.10**: A4 class 4-6-2 locomotive No. 2509 *Silver Link* at King's Cross Station, 16 June 1938. (SSPL/NRM)

A4 locomotives built to haul the train were painted a silver-grey colour. Within three weeks, the *Silver Link* had broken the British speed record by twice reaching 112½mph (181km/h) on its trial run of 27 September 1935.

The Doncaster works continued to build A4 Pacifics from late 1936 until 1938, and these were used to work two further streamlined trains that ran between King's Cross and Edinburgh, most notably the Coronation, which celebrated the accession of King George VI. This worked a punishing schedule from King's Cross to York with a full complement of nine coaches at a scheduled average speed of 71.9mph (116km/h), the highest ever required of British steam power. It was with six Coronation coaches and the dynamometer car that, on a test run on 3 July 1938, A4 No. 4468 *Mallard* (10.11) attained a top speed of 126mph (203km/h), a world record that has never been broken.

## ADVANCE OF THE COMBUSTION ENGINE

It was noted in Chapter 6 (see 6.13. page 82) how long the railway companies persisted with horses for the collection and delivery of goods. There was great pressure to reduce costs during the difficult financial years of the 1930s, but reducing costs required investment in equipment, and this constrained the advance of the combustion engine.

Following trials in 1931 at Bishopsgate and King's Cross, it was proposed to replace horses with tractors, twelve 'Cob' tractors substituting for eighteen single-horse teams. This rate of substitution was extended to a further 100 tractors, saving an estimated 10 per cent annually, which does not appear very significant and helps explain why the combustion engine failed to advance more rapidly. Similar cost savings were anticipated from substituting larger vehicles of 1–5 tons for single or paired horse teams.

Horse-drawn vehicles, or drays, were to be converted into rubber-tyred trailers for motor trailer working, which was considered more cost-effective than purchasing new trailers.

One impact of the advance of the combustion engine was the increasing traffic in containers; by 1930, King's Cross alone was handling 430 containers per month.

As early as 1928, Nigel Gresley had noted, in a letter to the CGM, that because of the very large increase in the LNER motor vehicle fleet, which he anticipated would soon reach 300, existing repair facilities had become quite inadequate. The position was most acute in the London area. Fifty-five lorries were stationed at King's Cross and, when not in use, stood under cover at the Potato Market (presumably in the service road, 8.7, page 101). There was a small garage on former gasworks land, inadequate as regards size, equipment and standing room, with no direct access from the goods yard.

Gresley suggested that the most efficient way to deal with lorries at King's Cross would be to provide cover for the whole fleet on the gasworks site, with direct roads access to Goods Way. Lorries could be run directly into a new garage and properly maintained, cleaned and prepared for use. A central workshop at Holloway, in which general overhauls and repairs to units could be properly undertaken, was also proposed.

**10.11**: Nigel Gresley's preserved three-cylinder streamline Pacifics in BR green, LNER silver and garter blue with *Mallard* on the right. (SSPL/NRM)

An alternative scheme requiring less investment and giving cover for eight lorries was prepared for the gasworks site. This would enable lorries to be brought in for washing, cleaning, oiling, greasing, and examination once a week, and would ensure they were properly maintained. The building was designed to be extended as required.

The need for economy dictated that neither scheme was implemented until 1934, when a new version of the less costly alternative was approved. The number of motor vehicles employed at King's Cross had by then reached 200 and the repair shop accommodation had become increasingly inadequate.

# KING'S CROSS GOODS STATION

There was very little money for improvement in goods handling for the first twelve years after grouping. Essentially the goods yard continued much as before until the mid-1930s with some changes in response to drastic declines in coal and grain traffic – the first for reasons described earlier, and grain because it had become an international commodity and most was now imported. Sugar largely took the place of grain, as sugar beet acreage in the eastern counties expanded.

A notable trend was the economic weakness of the northern manufacturing areas and the commercial and industrial growth of London in response to new technologies. This altered the balance of the inwards and outwards flow of goods, and the nature of the goods, with more smalls traffic.

From the mid-1930s, in response to government incentives in the form of cheap loans, the LNER embarked on a programme of investment in labour-reducing plant and equipment, helped by a workforce that, in the face of long dole queues, was relatively accommodating. It also built loading banks in the Train Assembly Shed, and a garage facility on the infilled Granary Basin.

But the major investment was the transposition of the Inwards and Outwards Sheds over 1937–38. It had been found that the Inwards Shed, with a capacity of 218 wagons, could accommodate only thirty-five wagons at unloading banks accessible to vehicles, resulting in frequent interruptions. The Outwards Shed, built over the former Coal and Stone Basin, was better equipped with, on the High Level, berthing accommodation for 161 wagons and, on the Low Level, for fifty-three wagons, making a total of 214 wagons, while the average number of outward wagons requiring to be dealt with was 370.

Inwards traffic would be dealt with in the Outwards Shed – both High and Low Levels – where unloading could proceed simultaneously from 214 wagons. Outwards traffic would be dealt with in the Inwards Shed, which would be adapted for this purpose by relaying practically all the sidings and removing the hydraulic turntables to enable adequate platform accommodation to be provided for the berthing of 200 wagons. Two electrically operated wagon traversers would be provided at the north end to expedite the transfer of wagons from siding to siding.

To improve the handling of empties in the northern sidings, the Loading Bank was extended by 228ft, providing facilities for dealing with eleven additional wagons, and making it practicable, with additional staff, for thirty-four wagons to be disposed of at one time.

# eleven

# Railway Folk

## COMPANY SERVANTS

Many jobs were required in the various departments of the company's terminus at King's Cross, including:

- Locomotive Department: clerical and supervisory, footplate men (drivers and firemen), cleaners, shed workshops (smiths, fitters, turners, boiler makers, carriage makers, wheelwrights, harness makers, tinmen, painters, and labourers).
- Traffic Department: booking clerks, ticket collectors, telephone and telegraph operators, clerks, passenger guards, goods guards, inspectors, foremen, shunters, porters.
- Goods and Coal Department: clerks, inspectors, foremen, checkers, loaders, callers off, porters and supernumerary men, lad porters, engine shunters, horse shunters, carmen, vanguards, lorry drivers, crane operators, fire watchmen, police.
- Hotels and Refreshments Department: chefs, kitchen hands, stewards, waiters, laundry workers, barrow boys.
- Horse Department: horse keepers, provender men, stable men, farriers.
- Public Omnibus Department: drivers, conductors, horse keepers, washers, harness cleaners.
- Potato Market: salesmen, porters, shunters, carmen, vanguards.

Images 11.1 to 11.3 show a sample of jobs. Other images that show railwaymen and ancillary workers are:

| | |
|---|---|
| 5.6 (page 66) | Craftsmen in front erecting shop |
| 5.7 (page 67) | The blacksmith's shop |
| 6.3 (page 75) | Provender men in stables |
| 8.1 (page 94) | Carmen and vanguards on delivery duty |
| 8.5 (page 99) | Warehouse workers in Potato Market |
| 12.8 (page 148) | Wheel tapper and A4 Pacific |

Job descriptions were further subdivided into a complicated structure of grades. The ladder that would take a cleaner to the top job of driving the royal train had dozens of rungs, a system that was predictable and awarded status as one progressed. Yet the same structure bred hierarchy, division and insularity.

The minutes of the various directors' committees provide almost no information on the numbers of company servants. GNR/LNER staff records were destroyed by the bomb that fell on the western office block of the station on 10–11 May 1941, flooding the basement. We must therefore be inventive in recreating the numbers of those who worked in the Railway Lands, using limited data.

Numbers increased steadily during the nineteenth century, reaching a peak of over 5,000 before the First World War. They will then have fallen for the next decade after amalgamation in 1923, before increasing from 1934 to the start of the Second World War, back up to around 5,000, as King's Cross became one of the hubs in a larger network.

| Year | Passenger Station, Hotel & Refreshment Department, Parcels, Omnibus Service | Goods & Coal Department, Horse Department | Locomotive Department | Potato Market, other independent traders, 5 per cent | Total |
|------|------|------|------|------|------|
| 1860 | 350 | 1,000 | 500 | 90 | 1,940 |
| 1875 | 650 | 1,600[1] | 800 | 150 | 3,200 |
| 1900 | 1,000[2] | 2,600[3] | 1,300 | 240 | 5,140 |
| 1937 | 1,200 | 2,400[4] | 1,200 | 240 | 5,040 |
| 1957 | 1,200[5] | 2,000 | 1,000[6] | 210 | 4,410 |
| 1975 | 800 | 1,000 | – | 90 | 1,890 |

**11.1**: A shunter using a pinch bar to move a goods wagon. (SSPL/NRM)

Notes
1. 3 July 1875, Goods Manager to General Manager, 'The number of men in the GN London Goods Department is about 1,598'.
2. J. Medcalf, April 1900.
3. Of which 700 carmen and vanguards, J. Medcalf, April 1900.
4. G.A. Roberts (1938).
5. 1,000 RMT members in King's Cross No.1 Branch, Ray Knight interviewed by Alan Dein for *King's Cross Voices*, with a 20 per cent allowance for non-union labour.
6. Personal communication, Peter N. Townend, January 2016.

## ORGANISATION OF LABOUR

The end of the First World War marked a turning point in employment. Large numbers of women had taken over many of the roles of railwaymen but, as men returned to the railway and jobs proved scarce, there were few places for women that were acceptable to the male workforce.

After 1919, there was almost no recruitment into the footplate grades until 1939. The government had introduced the National Conditions of Service, but under the conditions that prevailed after the 1923 amalgamation it was almost impossible for railwaymen to consolidate these gains, while employers, with the Company's owners in mind, were keen to erode them.

**11.2**: Chargeman Cleaner with gang of cleaners, mainly of Polish origin, cleaning the engine for the Elizabethan No. 60010 *Dominion of Canada*, with 60033 *Seagull* alongside. (P.N. Townend collection)

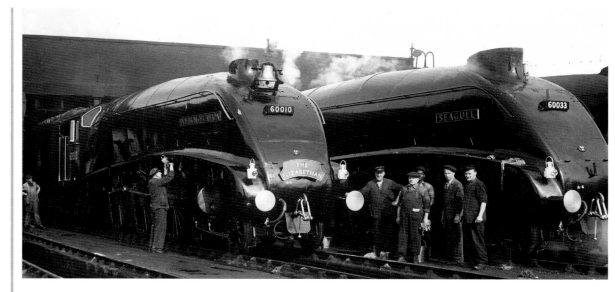

**11.3**: A shunter using hydraulic capstans to manoeuvre potato wagons. View east through Warehouse Nos. 21 and 22. The near column on the right is from the west arcade of the 1850 departure shed roof. The next column with spandrels supported the arcade between 1850 arrival and departure sheds, while against the rear wall is seen the east arcade of the 1850 arrival shed. (SSPL/NRM)

**11.4**: The Vigilants: Jim Swain carrying banner, Bob Lunniss marching behind with raincoat over shoulder. (Frank McKenna)

Initially the amalgamation introduced a period of union militancy with an ASLEF strike in 1924 and the General Strike of 1926. Both left railwaymen worse off than before.

The new company, the LNER, viewed the General Strike as an act of disloyalty by those that participated, and acted on this view, as described in the last chapter. With a weak economy and dole queues 2½ million long, rates of pay not only stagnated but railwaymen were enjoined to take a 2½ per cent cut to assist the Company. With pay and conditions deteriorating, apathy towards unions set in over the early 1930s.

A group of engine cleaners at King's Cross together with other railwaymen decided to combat this by setting up the Railway Vigilance Movement, founded in 1934 on the principle that 'the price of freedom is eternal vigilance'. This movement formed at local depot level and spread rapidly, working within the trade union branch, different grades in the depot setting up their own committees to work with the depot Vigilance Committee.

The Vigilants rapidly developed into a political movement of the left, aided by the high intellectual calibre of workshop floor leadership in which three King's Cross names were prominent: Francis Gates, Bob Lunniss and Jim Swain (11.4). Bob Lunniss served the London district council of ASLEF for twenty-five years as Assistant Secretary, Secretary and Chairman. Jim Swain was a representative for years and delegate to the Trades Union Congress.

The Vigilance Movement coincided with a period of increasing mechanisation, which threatened jobs. King's Cross depot was often blocked for a week by work-to-rule in the movement of locomotives around the new coaling plant. Urgent appeals were made by management to trade union head offices to calm down these Vigilance committee members. Between 1935 and 1939 there were more spasmodic stoppages and calls to work-to-rule than in all the years up to the General Strike. There was a strong belief that 'striking was good for the soul'.

## THE ARISTOCRACY OF THE WORKING CLASS

All train workings were assigned into 'links'. While King's Cross is associated with main line work on express trains, that work was restricted to the top three links. Most of the work was very mundane. 'Top Link', the most important passenger and express freight work, was only achieved after four decades of working lesser freight, shunting and shorter distance passenger work, and often depended on 'dead men's shoes', vacancies created by retirement. The strength of a driver's desire to reach the highest rung of the ladder made him amenable to deals that benefitted this small group of working-class elite, even at little immediate advantage to a man on a lower rung of the ladder.

By contrast, the junior link for firemen was 'Bottom Bunk', a small brick hut between the turntable and coaling tower. It was manned by three shifts of medically restricted drivers who took over the locomotives coming on shed. The division of labour through a multitude of separate tasks, and the separate loyalties these created, was responsible for a proliferation of separate premises both for work and messing.

Steam locomotives accumulated extraordinary amounts of dirt and grease during the course of the day, and there was an army of cleaners on hand, particularly for the more important passenger expresses. The dirty and dangerous cleaning work was described in Chapter 5.

Charlie Mayo (2012), who started his working life at Top Shed over 1952–54 as an engine cleaner aspiring to drive locomotives, provides a view of his prospects at that time.

First, the arguments for staying in the job.
- It's interesting. Any other job after this is going to be pretty dull.
- The money is not bad. I think eventually I'd even be able to save some.
- It's got some sort of future prospects – passenger trains, main line firing, etc.
- The blokes are interesting and mostly friendly.
- There is a lot to learn – a whole untapped world of experience and knowledge to learn.
- It would be politically right for me to stay. And politically interesting too, in the battles that so obviously lie somewhere ahead.
- And lastly, I like it, and feel that I'm really doing a man's job.

Against these ever so sound and reasonable arguments:

- One's whole life must be devoted to, and organised around, the job.
- One can't make any plans ahead.
- No social life is possible. It cuts one off from friends and the normal run of life.
- There is going to be a certain amount of redundancy some time in the future, and at such time, jobs outside will also be harder to come by.

Bob Lunniss could see the potential in the young man, but told him directly that he needed to be better informed before he could be of service to the union. He persuaded Charlie to apply to Ruskin College, Oxford to which he won a TUC scholarship. After two years at Oxford he won a scholarship to Trinity College, Cambridge and, to the disappointment of his sponsor, moved on into higher education.

But there were always new recruits to introduce to the cause (11.5). In the early 1950s, with an influx of West Indian workers, the so-called 'colour bar' dispute broke out when a black carriage cleaner was promoted to shunter. The shunters refused to accept him and, when the Company insisted, came out on strike.

11.5: New faces at King's Cross in the 1950s: Bob Lunniss and a new recruit. (Frank McKenna)

The colour bar survived until the end of steam, although progressively eroded by common class actions, particularly the solidarity created by the 1955 footplate-men's strike.

## HOUSING

Living locally, within a mile of the depot, was a condition of employment for those in key positions, notably the long-distance express drivers and firemen – who were often housed in railway-owned properties.

Stanley Buildings were built in 1864–65 for the Improved Industrial Dwellings Company, a philanthropic predecessor of the housing association, at a time when concern about public health and housing conditions was very vocal. Although the flats were small – originally four to a floor, later reduced to two – the five-storey buildings offered above-average accommodation for working people, with private sanitation, dust and ash chutes running down the stairwells and cast-iron balconies (11.6).

Left: **11.6**: The Stanley Buildings, south from Clarence Passage, May 2000. (Angela Inglis)

Right: **11.7**: Dancers on the wall, 1985. (Richard Holmes)

The affection residents had for these buildings is evident from the longevity of the mural of Fred Astaire and Ginger Rogers (11.7), created in the 1980s and still in fine condition ten years later.

Only one of the original five blocks that housed 104 families remains: of the four others, one was lost in wartime bombing, another was demolished for proposed road widening, the third was demolished for the CTRL works, and the fourth was demolished to allow the creation of Pancras Square and north–south through routes as part of King's Cross Central development.

The majority of remaining Stanley Buildings residents struck a deal with LCR, either receiving compensation or being rehoused.

The Culross Buildings of 1891–92 were built by the GNR to rehouse those displaced by the western expansion of the station into what became the Milk Dock site, parliamentary legislation that had recently passed imposing such rehousing requirements. However, they were primarily intended for railway employees, particularly those who were on call, and it seems likely that railwaymen soon formed most if not all the tenants. Flats were of two sizes, offering accommodation for both large families and couples.

The main building faced north onto Battle Bridge Road, providing forty flats over four floors (11.8). The basement was accessible from the railway side, and housed workshops and mess rooms. It ran alongside the Milk Dock, or former Express Dairy Rail Depot, accessed from Cheney Road (11.9).

After the end of steam a very different group, mainly younger people, moved into Stanley Buildings, who, typical of the era, saw themselves as the punk generation in friendly contrast to the older residents, who they regarded as the hippy generation. They characterised their time there as having a strong sense of community, with doors left open and a common roof garden that became a noted social gathering area and party venue. The Mission had gone and the Culross residents took over Culross Hall, which they could now hire out for gigs and, for a while, as a kick-boxing school.

The residents' association was very active, not least because it was well funded, initially by a levy on the rent but later from fees received from film and advertising companies. The edgy industrial landscape, combining decaying brick buildings, walls and gasholders with the last cobbled Victorian street in London, proved irresistible to the media.

**11.9**: Milk Depot north platform showing the railway siding that was formerly for unloading milk churns from trains, view from the south-west. Culross Buildings are on the left, and the external wooden staircase to Culross Mission Hall was used by railwaymen as a shortcut to Battle Bridge Road and thus to the goods yard or Top Shed. Käthe Strenitz, pen and wash, 1977, courtesy of Käthe Strenitz Estate. (LMA)

# MISSIONS, SOCIAL ACTIVITIES AND SOCIAL SECURITY

Social security was a major concern for railwaymen from the start. In 1853 some eighty employees of the Goods Department wrote to the General Manager, Seymour Clarke, asking that a provident society be formed for their benefit. They prefaced this request by informing him that they had been given to understand when they joined the Company that they would subscribe to a provident society, and some had consequently discontinued paying other societies and were regretting their decision. They noted that nearly every pay day they were asked to assist one or other fellow workman who had fallen sick. It is not clear how successful this request proved.

Lord Culross, the GNR Chairman, was a Christian and interested in railway staff hearing the Gospel. The Culross Mission was established in Culross Hall in 1898 for the moral welfare of residents and neighbours. Culross Hall had been built about ten years earlier as part of the carriage and wagon department, and the Culross Building was joined to this smaller building at Culross Hall's western end. The Mission Hall provided a common meeting place for various groups of men who had been meeting as Christians on railway premises. The GNR appointed a London City Missionary to be in charge.

The Mission produced a monthly magazine, the *Culross Hall Magazine*, which provided a popular way for railway staff to learn what was happening outside their immediate circle. Culross became known up and down the line because of the magazine. In the age before unions the Mission provided financial help to those in need as well as advice of a pastoral nature. The heads of the Mission were highly respected as anyone who fell on hard times could seek their help.

The Mission ran camps at the seaside and Christmas parties for the widows and children of men who had been killed on the railway, many crushed in the shunting yard. Out of that grew the Widows and Orphans Fund. There were collections all over the station and its various ancillary depots. The London City Mission would help but most of the support came from the railway staff.

In the early days the Railway Temperance Movement was associated with Culross Mission, the missionary in charge being the chair of the committee. It was run by working men, committed Christians, who wanted to encourage temperance and keep men off drink. There were competitions throughout the year with prizes awarded.

# twelve

# To the End of Steam

## SECOND WORLD WAR

Preparations for the possible outbreak of war started in 1938 with the following measures:

- appointment of air raid precautionary (ARP) officers by area and district
- training of selected staff in ARP measures
- planning for protection of vital installations
- provision of splinter-proof shelters.

The LNER procured sand and materials, making sandbags in their workshops for both their own needs and those of the LMS Railway. A Special Committee was convened to take responsibility for addressing lighting restrictions, emergency repairs and other measures in the event of enemy action.

The Chief General Manager, Ralph Wedgwood, set out two ARP guidelines that would apply throughout the coming conflict:

i.  Railway companies would bear the whole cost of 'good employer' precautions.
ii. Government would set up a fund to defray the cost of other precautionary measures that were sanctioned by the Ministry of Transport.

A contract was let to W&C French in April 1939 to construct air raid shelters within a ten-week time frame.

Stop gates were installed on the Regent's Canal on both sides of Gasworks Tunnel to limit flooding of the tunnel in the event of a bomb strike. They were closed each night during the war.

An early casualty was King's Cross Metropolitan Station, which closed on 16 October 1940 because of bomb damage.

The goods yard sustained major damage from an air raid on 9 November 1940. The panorama (12.1) shows the eastern wall of the main goods offices (now Regeneration House) destroyed, together with bomb damage to the Eastern Transit Shed (then the Outwards Shed) and to the Road Motor Depot that stood in the Granary forecourt, seen on the left. The evidence for this damage can still be seen in the reconstruction of part of the façade of the Eastern Transit Shed and the shrapnel damage to the east wall of the Granary.

The same air raid also saw York Road Station severely damaged (12.2).

**12.1**: A panoramic view of damage to Eastern Transit Shed and other buildings nearby on 9 November 1940, C.C.B. Herbert. (National Archives)

**12.2**: Damage at York Road Station on 9 November 1940 looking east towards York Way. There is a type B air raid shelter on left, C.C.B. Herbert. (National Archives)

The goods yard suffered two further attacks, on 30 January and 18 February 1941. Damage was slight but five railwaymen were injured in the first attack.

Several bombs fell in the Top Shed area, but only one did any serious damage. A high-explosive bomb fell on the 'Continent', the sidings that ran along the south side of the Running Shed, demolishing part of the wall and roof of the Running Shed as well as destroying some track and damaging several locomotives (12.3).

The most extensive damage as a result of enemy action was sustained on the last night of the Blitz, on 10–11 May 1941, when three LNER London terminals, King's Cross, Liverpool Street and Marylebone, were hit. At King's Cross a high-explosive bomb struck the western office block facing No. 10 platform. There were nine fatalities, four of the company's men and five soldiers. A length of about 75ft (23m) between the Booking Hall and the Footbridge

**12.3**: Damage to the main line Running Shed. (SSPL/NRM)

was destroyed, as well as five bays of the station roof. The collapse of the roof girders blocked the four western platforms. The bomb damage caused flooding of the basement, destroying all the records kept there.

On 26 June 1944, at 1.15 p.m., a pilotless aircraft fell in Tiber Street, just off York Way on the north side of the Regent's Canal, causing extensive damage to windows in the goods yard and bringing down some ceilings in the General Offices. The King's Cross area was hit by three further V1 flying bombs in 1944. Some of the most heavily damaged areas were the streets of terraced housing immediately north of the canal and east of York Way, where two V1 flying bombs landed within 500 yards of each other.

## RAILWAY LANDS SEEN FROM THE AIR

The aerial photograph shown in 12.4 was flown by the RAF in 1945–46 as part of Operation Review, using equipment built up during the war to take high-definition 1:5,000 scale photographs.

The impact on residential properties of V1s that fell nearby can be seen in the reconstruction that followed the war. The aerial photograph shows the clearance of these streets of houses (Dennis Street, Tiber Street and Oakland Street), and the start of construction of social housing.

**12.4**: King's Cross Railway Lands, aerial photograph taken by the RAF 1945–46. (Getmapping)

The damage sustained by the northern wing of the western range of offices at the main passenger station can be clearly seen. The building was not reinstated to its original form until the construction of the new concourse.

The exceptional image definition allows us to discern a retaining wall at the top of the grassed bank west of the Passenger Locomotive Depot, immediately west of which is a line of seven air raid shelters running north–south. Only the ventilation shafts are visible.

The image shows that the gasworks site was still largely undeveloped by LNER. There were piggeries just south of Goods Way, and the land had been cleared for what was intended as a Motor Repair Depot. But the budget had only stretched to a line of stables/garages and petrol pumps that ran along the boundary with the still active gasholders, and to a garage and motor repair shop along Battle Bridge Road. The area was being used for parking trucks.

There are no traces of the Midland Roundhouse, which had been demolished in 1931. The line of potato warehouses along York Way is very clearly discernible.

12.5: No. 4472 *Flying Scotsman* down train approaching Copenhagen Tunnel, observed by trainspotters from the location made famous in *The Ladykillers*. Taken on 1st May 1968, on the fortieth anniversary of its first non-stop run, after its preservation by Alan Pegler, Colin Gifford. (Museum of London)

## TRAINSPOTTING

Trainspotting is a pastime almost as old as the railways themselves. As so well described by Simon Bradley (2016), it grew rapidly before the Second World War before becoming a craze in the 1950s, and waning after the end of steam. It had been stimulated by nationalisation, which created a single pool of locomotives with a unified numbering system. Armed with one of the many publications produced to support the craze, the trainspotter in the 1950s may be compared to a birdwatcher in an extraordinarily wildlife rich landscape.

King's Cross Platform 10 was a noted spotting location for watching the outward and inward movement of dozens of trains, as was the approach to Copenhagen Tunnel where the excitement of seeing, hearing, smelling and feeling powerful steam locomotives as they pounded up Holloway Bank was itself a strong stimulus, described in the Billy Osborne interview in Chapter 9, and brilliantly captured on camera by Colin Gifford (12.5).

## MOTOR REPAIR DEPOT

Construction of a motor repair depot on the former gasworks site had been strongly urged since 1928 by Nigel Gresley, but what was built pre-war was relatively modest. It was not until 1955 that a more substantial facility was provided. This was built on the embankment opposite York Road Station overlooking the Passenger Locomotive Depot and approach tracks into the passenger station (12.6).

To prepare the site, the piggeries along Goods Way and seven air raid shelters on the site of the planned new buildings were demolished.

The Motor Repair Depot comprised a main shop of six bays, a paint shop in a seventh bay, a boiler house and ancillary offices, mess room, and private car bay.

The buildings survived until around 2000. By then they had long been abandoned as a repair depot, but had found other less official uses, as described in Chapter 15.

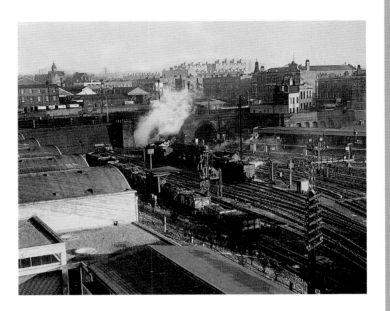

## LAST DAYS OF THE STEAM LOCOMOTIVES

The work required to maintain steam locomotives in service was described in Chapter 5. The pride that continued to be taken in the appearance of the express locomotives is manifest in David Shepherd's

12.6: Motor Repair Depot from the south-west, looking towards York Road, January 1957. (Irwell Press)

12.7: 'Scotsman '34' – *Flying Scotsman* at Top Shed in the mid-1930s, oil on canvas, painted *c.*1964, David Shepherd. (Courtesy of Avril Shepherd)

'Scotsman '34', painted in the mid-1960s after the closure of Top Shed (12.7). David Shepherd (1931–2017) had a passion for steam that led him to buy two main line steam locomotives from BR in 1967 and the station at Cranmore with rail road, building a Victorian reproduction locomotive shed and founding the East Somerset Railway (Shepherd, 1983).

The final words should perhaps come from Peter Townend (1989), Shedmaster in the 1950s, who in the introduction to his book *Top Shed* places his own nostalgic regrets about steam locomotives in context:

After spending a number of years trying to overcome some of the problems associated with their operation, the end was inevitable. People generally were not prepared to accept the dirt, grime and smoke associated with steam traction and there were many unpleasant tasks which had to be carried out in primitive conditions at depots, which few men really wanted to do.

The unequal relationship of steam locomotive and railway employee is epitomised in the

**12.8**: The wheel tapper waits, hammer in hand, as A4 Pacific No. 60034 *Lord Farringdon* eases an up express into King's Cross in summer 1961, E.H. Sawford. (Transport Treasury)

image of the wheeltapper and the streamlined A4 Pacific (12.8). A wheeltapper was employed to check the integrity of train wheels, examined by tapping wheels with a long-handled hammer and listening to the sound made. The scene on the approach to the platforms at King's Cross in 1961 is intimately associated with the steam age.

Top Shed closed on 16 June 1963. Scheduled steam trains stopped running into King's Cross, although steam locomotives continued to arrive sporadically when substituted for a failed Deltic diesel. The buildings at Top Shed were demolished soon after the shed closed, before industrial archaeologists could make a record of what had stood there. There is now no trace of what had once been one of the most important steam depots in the country.

There remains a tremendous nostalgia for steam among those who worked with it. Charlie Mayo expresses this, as well as recognising the inevitability of the end, in *Night Freight*, written in 1954 when he was employed as a trainee fireman at Top Shed (Mayo, 2012).

THE KING'S CROSS STORY: 200 YEARS OF HISTORY IN THE RAILWAY LANDS

### Night Freight

Johnny Fireman swings a shovel
On the freight train through the night.
Johnny Driver eyes the signals
Watching through the rain for the danger light.

Through the night the freight train thunders,
Throwing fire against the sky
And the light from the engine cab is blazing
Like a dragon's angry eye.

Johnny Driver eyes the signals
As they loom and disappear
And the smoke lies flat along the boiler
As he gives her full power with the road all clear.

Strain on eye and strain on ear-drum,
Strain on fire and strain on steel.
Strain on muscle on the rocking footplate,
Strain to the rhythm of the pounding wheel.

People in their beds can hear the thunder
And howling whistle down the line,
And young boys turn in their beds and dream
As the silence closes in behind.

Johnny Fireman slings his shovel,
Johnny Driver takes the strain,
With one hand controls the power
As they rumble in the yards again.

In the drizzle of a cold wet morning
As the rails begin to gleam
They come slowly into the goods yard,
Huffing and puffing in a shuffle of steam.

It was familiar as Monday morning,
Soon to be forgotten as years roll on.
Only the men who lived it, worked it
Knew of the feeling for a life
That's gone.

## END OF CANAL FREIGHT

As far as the transhipment of goods and minerals at King's Cross was concerned, none of the basins, docks and wharves had been operating since the end of the First World War. Commercial traffic on the Regent's Canal was, however, still buoyant in the early 1950s (12.9), with almost 750,000 tons carried in 1954. But by the mid-1960s traffic had declined drastically, and a series of government white papers accepted the concept of an amenity network, formalised in the Transport Act 1968. This stimulated the opening of the towpath from Hampstead Road to Islington Tunnel, which was later extended to Limehouse Dock.

## NEW DIESELS AND ELECTRICS

A new Diesel Locomotive Maintenance Depot was built at Finsbury Park, some 2 miles north of King's Cross, opening in 1960 on the site of the former Clarence Yard freight depot.

It was planned to provide regular maintenance for some 180 diesel locomotives from 200hp (149kW) shunters to the largest main line 'Deltic' locomotive of 3,300hp (2,460kW), the most powerful single-unit diesel locomotive built at that time in the country.

**Above left: 12.9**: A 7hp petrol-driven tractor towing a barge above St Pancras Locks, with the Western Goods Shed (Inwards Shed) in the middle distance left, 30 July 1953. (CRT)

**Above right: 12.10**: Deltic No. 55002 *King's Own Yorkshire Light Infantry* departs King's Cross on 12 June 1975, powering the *Aberdonian* on its 523 mile (842km) journey to the Granite City and passes Class 31/4 No. 31407 on pilot duties. (Brian Morrison)

**Opposite bottom: 12.13**: 'King's Cross Away Day Girls' on Goods Way, gouache on paper, 1979. (Anne Howeson)

**12.11**: King's Cross, 21 September 1991. From left to right: No. 91018 heads the 08.00 for Edinburgh; No. 90023 will power the 08.05 special to the same destination; No. 43050 leads the 08.30, also for the Scottish capital; and a Mk4 DVT (Driving Van Trailer – a purpose-built control car that allows the driver to operate a locomotive at the opposite end of a train) leads the 08.10 for Leeds. (Brian Morrison)

Deltics were the premier locomotives of the East Coast Main Line from their introduction in 1961 to their withdrawal in 1982, transforming the performance times of trains such as the *Flying Scotsman*. Among the best known was Deltic 55002, *The King's Own Yorkshire Light Infantry* (12.10), affectionately known as 'KOYLI', with its own devoted following and a home now in the Great Hall at the National Railway Museum. Some of its successors, diesel and electric, are shown in 12.11.

It was only with the HST 125s that King's Cross Station at last became adequate for its traffic.

## STREETWALKERS

As we learned in Chapter 1, the area around present day King's Cross has had a poor environment and a reputation for crime for a very long time. More recently, in the nineteenth century, it was associated with the wholesale clearance of poorer communities to make way for railways. While these clearances may have played well to middle-class sensibilities, they accentuated the deprivation and overcrowding in the surrounding residential areas, and turned St Pancras into the most densely populated part of London.

The railways created numerous transient workers – drivers, firemen and train crews – that had to find overnight accommodation far from home, and many found temporary shelter in the King's Cross area, close to the stations and goods yards where they worked. There were many other transients from all over the country passing through the area in search of employment and accommodation. This transient population created its own needs.

Prostitution had operated in the area for a long time, but grew through the 1970s and 1980s, with drugs becoming an increasing problem, before efforts were made progressively to clear the area or, as some might think, to move the problem elsewhere. At its height, it was quite open and indiscreet, with girls lining both sides of Goods Way, much as depicted in Neil Jordan's 1986 film *Mona Lisa* (12.12), which identifies the street scene as King's Cross. Seen though a car windscreen, streetwalkers and kerb crawlers are part of an underworld of vice and criminality.

Below top: **12.12**: Streetwalkers on Goods Way, extract from *Mona Lisa*, directed by Neil Jordan. (Visual Icon)

Anne Howeson (2009) roamed the streets with sketchbook and pencil over three decades from the 1970s, often at night. Attracted by the no man's land of Goods Way and the maze of streets and buildings, she created a symbolic vision of transition from gritty, colourful and downbeat to new, grey and impersonal. The 'Away Day Girls' she drew (12.13, page 151) came up to London from Yorkshire to find business, especially during the era of the Yorkshire Ripper in Leeds. This led to a major row between the girls and their respective 'minders' in Pancras Road until an 'agreement' had been hammered out between the relevant firms who controlled the business. As a result, the London girls worked one side of the road and the Yorkshire girls the other.

As well as Goods Way and Pancras Road, ladies of the night operated in Camley Street and Cheney Road, behind Stanley Buildings, where they had access to the Milk Dock, at that time the Motorail Depot (13.13, page 160), from which a night train carried cars to the north while their owners took the overnight passenger train.

Local residents interviewed for *King's Cross Voices* over 2004–07 were quite happy to provide both prurient detail and humour, many describing the use by sex workers of passages leading to their flats. One describes the front door of his ground floor flat shaking, and when he opened it the couple fell in!

The arrest of the Director of Public Prosecutions for kerb crawling in Goods Way in October 1991 made many lurid newspaper headlines, one of which was adopted by an indignant waterside resident of Goods Way Moorings who changed her address to 'The Road to Ruin and Despair'.

12.14: NFC Freightliner depot at King's Cross, 1967. (SSPL/NRM)

## FREIGHTLINER OPERATIONS

The railways entered a boom period for traffic after the Second World War, which was handled under great difficulties until the ASLEF strike of 1955, following which there was a rapid decline of traffic.

With the benefit of hindsight, it appears extraordinary that in such a vulnerable business there was not more cooperation and less confrontation, as the latter seriously disadvantaged both labour and management.

By the early 1960s the writing was clearly on the wall for wagonload traffic and by 1970 almost all the 'sundries/small' traffic associated with the London depots had vanished. One of the recommendations of the infamous Beeching 1963 report *The Reshaping of British Railways* was the setting up of a national network of terminals served by express freightliner trains that would replace the outdated system of wagon loading.

The York Way terminal (also known as Maiden Lane) at King's Cross was the pioneer depot for what became the Freightliner brand. The first revenue-earning Freightliner trains ran between York Way and Glasgow on 15 November 1965.

Freightliner operations could be divided into the movement of containers by rail and the transfer of containers at terminals such as York Way to road vehicles (12.14, opposite) for cartage and delivery (C&D) to end customers. While investments were made in both sides of the operation, C&D was the less profitable and advantageous side for the rail industry, which preferred to spend investment capital on the Freightliner rail-side component and the terminals.

The problem of poor loadings and lack of return on investment drove the government towards promoting open terminals that could be used by private hauliers. This was seen by the NUR as a threat to the cartage side of the business and to the livelihood of the drivers the union represented. After much arm twisting by Barbara Castle, Transport Minister, and many assurances on pay and redundancy, they finally accepted the principle of free access to terminals.

The debates that led to the Freightliner operation exposed many of the fault lines of a declining rail business and how to make it profitable:

- road vs rail – a complex set of political, commercial and union loyalties
- public vs private operators
- dispersal of depots vs concentration into a few larger more efficient depots
- unions vs Railway Board
- the flexible culture required to make a complex system like Freightliner work to a precise timetable vs a culture of frequent disruption and 'work to rule'.

The 1968 Transport Act established Freightliner as a separate company from BR, operating as part of the National Freight Corporation, itself part of National Carriers to which King's Cross goods depot was transferred under the 1968 Transport Act. While it took ownership of the containers, BR provided the locomotive traction, the terminals and the wagons under a lease arrangement.

It soon became clear that Freightliner's future lay in developing its core routes, with longer and more frequent trains serving a smaller number of regional terminals. The cull of marginal depots began in 1986 with the closure of King's Cross, which by then was handling only a nightly service to and from Edinburgh. The operation gradually concentrated on moving full trainloads of sea containers between a small number of ports and inland distribution terminals.

## READY-MIXED CONCRETE YARD

The northern end of the site had developed for aggregates and ready-mixed concrete production, with several companies based there and receiving inward materials by rail. The site is shown on 13.15 on page 161.

# thirteen

# Industrial Ruins

## THE POWER OF RUINS

The demolition of Top Shed and the increasing dereliction of the Railway Lands over the subsequent two decades created a landscape that both attracted and repelled, according to one's attachment to a sense of order.

At the start of the railway era in the mid-nineteenth century, the railway companies had played on middle-class perceptions and their fears of the dirt and diversity of the poorer areas that they wanted to demolish. Now that the Railway Lands were themselves the cause of middle-class angst, powerful vested interests could promote the 'wasteland' discourse and harness the fears and prejudice that this engendered for economic ends.

Local and national authorities saw such areas as blighted, associated with crime and a threat to neighbouring communities. The views of the communities themselves were more nuanced. Some saw a weed-infested wasteland, whereas others saw a potential nature reserve and wildlife habitat. Craftsmen saw workshops that could be colonised at affordable cost, whereas other professions saw buildings that stood in the way of redevelopment. To some the ruins were an increasingly painful reminder of industrial decline, whereas industrial archaeologists could see the affirmation of a past that needed proper explanation. And while many saw an abandoned and derelict landscape, others saw spaces for play, whether warehouse raves or go-kart tracks.

Artists felt the power and saw the beauty in the industrial ruins. Prominent among such artists was Käthe Strenitz, whose drawings make up this chapter as well as appearing on the cover, in the title pages and in Chapters 9 and 11. Anne Howeson's drawing features in Chapter 12 and Marianne Fox-Ockinga's in Chapters 11 and 15. Angela Inglis' photographs and poems are distributed in Chapters 11, 14 and 15.

**KÄTHE STRENITZ** was born in 1923 in Jablonec (Gablonz), in the Sudeten part of Czechoslovakia into a relatively prosperous and forward thinking Jewish family that was well integrated with the local German community. Her mother moved in intellectual circles that embraced the famous Vienna-based psychologist, Alfred Adler, who advised her on childrearing.

Her early enthusiasm for, and education in, art was spurred by the family's move to Prague in 1938. Here she was exposed to avant-garde ideas and influences while attending art college.

In March 1939 the Germans occupied Prague, and within weeks she found herself, aged 16, on a Nicholas Winton inspired *kindertransport* train to England, leaving her family – parents and brother – behind.

Her arrival and wait for collection at Liverpool Street left her with an abiding impression of large, brooding, dark industrial landscapes, which echoed through much of her subsequent work.

Her early experience of England during the war was very mixed, some of it spent in Kent in agricultural work, from picking fruit and vegetables to milking goats and ploughing with horses. Meanwhile her drawings were brought to the attention of Oskar Kokoschka, on whose recommendation she was awarded a scholarship to Regent Street Polytechnic in 1942. This did not work out well either financially or from an aesthetic viewpoint, the instructors having been recalled from retirement. She went back to war work, living in a Czech hostel where she met her future husband, Otto Fischel, whom she married in 1943. They had a daughter in 1950.

She returned to the Regent Street Polytechnic in the mid-1950s, where she was taught by David Smith, a painter/engraver, who asked her to join him, and with whom she later shared a studio. She studied wood engraving, woodcarving and woodcutting, making woodcuts of her drawings for the next two decades, until the physical effort proved too great.

Her husband meanwhile had bought a derelict tripe factory in Market Road, at the north end of Copenhagen Tunnel, which he converted and extended into a factory for plastic injection mouldings. This provided Käthe with a base from which to explore the surrounding industrial landscapes at King's Cross and St Pancras. The gasholders and warehouses were fascinating as subjects, as was the industrial detritus that littered these spaces. She roamed along Regent's Canal in both directions, down to the City, dockland and the river,

and up to Hampstead Road Locks, until she started to feel unsafe and exposed to vandals. She also drew many of the residential side streets in the neighbourhood. Several scenes remain unidentified.

On a visit to Wales, she drew coal mines and villages near Aberfan after the disaster. These are in the National Library of Wales. She has a separate body of work concentrating on the human figure.

Although her most successful medium was woodcuts, she also painted in oils. Käthe's first exhibition was at the Ben Uri Gallery in March 1961, and she exhibited there, at Camden Arts Centre and at other galleries until a joint exhibition with David Smith at Boundary Gallery in September 1990. She exhibited regularly at the Bankside Gallery, was elected a Fellow of the Royal Society of Painter-Printmakers in 1972, and received the Lord Mayor's Award for woodcuts in 1973. Her woodcuts and oils may be found in many museums, galleries and archives, including the Guildhall, Ashmolean, Graves Art Gallery, Camden Local Studies and Archives and Islington Local History Centre.

But her favourite medium was pen and ink, often with a colour wash. She regarded these black and white drawings as better suited to the landscapes she was drawing. The largest collection of such drawings, over 200 in number, remains uncatalogued and unexhibited at London Metropolitan Archives, to which her drawings were transferred in 1989 and in 2017 to ensure they remained together as a body of work.

As she entered her tenth decade, the deep traumas left by the holocaust were ever present, in mourning her next of kin and in preserving the artistic legacy of long lost friends, particularly Peter Kien. She died on 29 August 2017.

## KÄTHE STRENITZ'S RAILWAY LANDS

Her base was her husband's plastics factory in Market Road, just off York Way, overlooking the northern portal of Copenhagen Tunnel (9.9, page 115). With some help from factory employees acting as drivers, she roamed over the King's Cross and St Pancras Railway Lands, along the Regent's Canal, up to Caledonian Road and over the streets of Camden, Islington and other areas.

Her fascination with industrial landscapes stemmed from her arrival in 1939 at Liverpool Street Station from Prague at age 16 (see box above). The large, very black and gloomy station left an indelible impression on her consciousness.

She believed in a limited subject matter and found much of interest in the decommissioned areas of the goods yard. She painted in oils and made woodcuts on a huge restored Victorian press that required an extension to her house. While woodcuts proved her most successful medium commercially, she mostly worked in pencil, ink and wash or charcoal, creating black and white drawings, with a few watercolours, capturing the industrial nature of the subject.

The sixteen images in this chapter have all been provided courtesy of the Käthe Strenitz Estate.

The following passages are an extract from *King's Cross Voices*, around 2005. The interviewer was Sue Kinder.

Could you tell me how you came to be working in King's Cross?

I was always interested in the decline of the industrial scene and when my husband started a factory in Market Road near King's Cross I had an ideal place from where to work. I tried to record as much of the neighbourhood which included the canal, railway, and the general landscape around King's Cross.

The factory before, it was in a ruinous state, the old one, they pulled it down. It used to be a tripe factory so you could still see bits of bones. It was owned by, I don't remember, I think he said Hammonds that had tripe shops all over London.

That must have been something for a Jewish couple to be owning a former tripe factory, must have been unusual.

Yes, facing the railway line and the film, 'The Ladykillers' was shot there, except for the little house but otherwise the location of the film is a lot of my subject that appeared in this film. The back wall of the factory is in this film which is really nice.

When did Otto buy the factory?

I don't remember when he bought the factory but the drawings are mostly from 30 years ago. Over several years, but I don't have any dates for the drawings and I haven't dated them which is another thing.

You were inspired to do the drawings because of the industrial landscape?

It was interesting because when I arrived in England I arrived in Liverpool Street Station and this visual impression of the station was so strong because it was incredibly large and terribly black and it imprinted itself on my consciousness so that ever after I was looking for this sort of scene, whether it was conscience or not I don't know but this is what happened. I can trace it to that.

You said you liked drawing at the end of the platforms.

Yes, I particularly liked King's Cross Station once they were out of commission. There were wonderful bits of old buckets and stuff standing around. You hardly ever saw any people incidentally where I was drawing because these platforms were never in use anymore and quite derelict. So it was rare that you met someone.

Occasional guard or train driver? Tell me the story again about the man moving the train.

Well that was very nice because that was the end of one of the King's Cross platforms where only sort of industrial trains came in and bits, I don't think it had any function anymore anyway. A train driver brought a train in and stopped bang right in front of my view. He came over to me and I said excuse me, you are standing in front of my subject so he said oh, I'm going to move the train. He moved the train back and after about half an hour he came and said have you finished? I said yes.

**13.3**: The site of the former Potato Market (in the foreground) after demolition of warehouses 24–36; East Handyside Canopy is on the right with spandrels from original Temporary Passenger Station of 1850. The ventilation shaft serves Gasworks Tunnel. The three telegraph poles that cut through the canopy date from 1897. Käthe Strenitz, pen and wash, 1977. (LMA)

**13.4**: The view south under East Handyside Canopy, with the Midland Goods Shed in the centre and West Handyside Canopy on the right; on the far right is the Eastern Transit Shed east flank wall, with arched openings. Käthe Strenitz, pen and wash, 1977. (LMA)

**13.5**: West Handyside Canopy, south end, looking north, with Eastern Transit Shed on the left and Midland Goods Shed on the right. Käthe Strenitz, pen and wash, 1977. (LMA)

Right: **13.6**: East Handyside Canopy, north end looking north. The Potato Market is on the right beyond the tracks (warehouses 4–23 and 37–38 survived the demolition of 24–36); Ebonite Tower is in the distance; West Handyside Canopy is beyond the columns on the left. Käthe Strenitz, pen and wash, 1977. (LMA)

**13.7**: Wharf Road looking west to the gasholders and Coal and Fish Offices. Käthe Strenitz, pen and wash, 1988. (LMA)

**13.8**: Wharf Road from the Plimsoll Viaduct looking south. From the left: the Eastern Coal Drops (latterly Bagley's glass bottle warehouse); the Coal and Fish Offices with the gasholders behind; the arches under Wharf Road that formerly provided stabling; St Pancras train shed; and more gasholders. Käthe Strenitz, pen and wash, 1977. (LMA)

**13.9**: Wharf Road looking north-west, with the traverser of the former Cambridge Street Coal Drops on the left; the 1899 Western Goods Shed in the background; the former Western Coal Drops with Berlin Bank extending to the right; and the Plimsoll Viaduct, rebuilt in iron on brick arches in 1899, immediately in front of the former coal drops. Käthe Strenitz, pen and wash, 1977. (LMA))

**13.10**: The demolition of Cambridge Street (now Camley Street) Coal Drops. The canal is on the left, Camley Street is on the right. In the background is the Midland Grand Hotel, completed in 1876 to designs by Sir George Gilbert Scott, while the multi-roofed building on the canal bend is the former Wiggins Stables. The area being demolished is now Camley Street Natural Park. Käthe Strenitz, watercolour, 1977. (LMA)

**13.11**: Camley Street, south end, looking south. The Midland Coal Drops on the right were demolished in the 1960s to create a refuse dump. One of the Stanley Buildings can be seen in the distance. Käthe Strenitz, pen and wash, 1977. (LMA)

**13.12**: The view south from St Pancras Locks to the Coal and Fish Offices. The retaining wall supports Wharf Road and the goods yard and features windows to the arches behind that formerly stabled some 120 horses. Two bays of the former Wiggins Stables can be seen on the south bank, at the bend in the canal. Käthe Strenitz, watercolour, 1976. (LMA)

**13.13**: The entrance to Motorail Depot, Cheney Street. Stanley Buildings are on the left. This street, and neighbouring ones, were much used by film and advertisement makers seeking a Victorian setting due to their granite setts paving. Motorail was the brand name for BR's long-distance services that carried passengers' cars; it began in 1955 between King's Cross and Perth, and the sidings were used to unload Motorail vans. The service transferred to Euston in May 1988. Käthe Strenitz, pen and wash, *c.* 1985. (LMA)

**13.14**: Motorail Depot. Looking north-east, the Culross Building is on the left, alongside Culross Mission Hall. Käthe Strenitz, pen and wash, 1985. (LMA)

**13.15**: Concrete yard at the north end of Railway Lands. Käthe Strenitz, pen and wash, 1977. (LMA)

**13.16**: The York Way Viaduct over the goods yard sidings. Five Arch Viaduct, through which the goods and locomotive yard lines ran, is on the left. Käthe Strenitz, pen and wash, 1977. (LMA)

# fourteen

# Conflict over the Railway Lands

## TESTING THE WATERS

The former Cambridge Street Coal Drops were demolished in 1977 (13.10). The Greater London Council (GLC) bought the site, just over 2 acres of land, in 1981 to make a coach/lorry park. The GLC Ecology Unit and London Wildlife Trust, part of a growing urban biodiversity movement, opposed these plans, as did the local community. It was decided to develop the land into Camley Street Natural Park (CSNP), a permanent local nature reserve.

Work started at the end of 1983 largely with local volunteers. They dug the pond, watched the liner and water go in, planted the trees, seeded the meadows and mulched the site. It may have taken longer

**14.1**: Camley Street Natural Park in spring 1985, shortly before its official opening. (Richard Holmes)

**14.2**: Camley Street Natural Park looking north in February 2004, Angela Inglis. (Courtesy of Rob Inglis)

**14.3**: Reedmace, November 2005, Angela Inglis. (Courtesy of Rob Inglis)

to build with community involvement, but it created a strong sense of ownership. The official opening was on 7 May 1985 by Mayor Ken Livingstone.

However, British Rail's plans to bring the new international station to King's Cross included a line coming in a covered tunnel straight through Camley Street. Barely three years after opening the CSNP, a large campaign, involving all the local schools, had to be triggered to protect it.

When eventually the British Rail project was abandoned, and it was decided to take the Channel Tunnel Rail Link (CTRL) to St Pancras, the gasholders that formed the backdrop to CSNP (14.1) were disassembled or demolished. Another consequence of CTRL was a drop in the level of the road at the junction of Goods Way with Camley Street, both roads falling to this junction. There is now a retaining wall at this southern corner, and the CSNP is more visible, appearing to be on a hill as you approach it from St Pancras Way.

The St Pancras Waterpoint, designed by the office of Sir George Gilbert Scott and built in 1872, lay alongside the railway line just behind the gasholders, but in the path of CTRL. It was sliced into sections and moved 700m north-east to the end of the park and now forms part of its backdrop. The magnificent iron gates to the site were originally those for Somers Town goods yard, now the site of the British Library.

Initially the CSNP served schools all over London but when the GLC was abolished, Camden took over part of the funding with the London Wildlife Trust and the focus since then is on Camden schools.

The park lies alongside the Regent's Canal (14.1), which feeds the pond and marshy areas with water. When the canal flooded, it washed fish into the pond from the canal, and they have remained and flourished. The large pond has a platform that can accommodate a whole class for pond dipping. Children catch newts, frogs, tadpoles and small fish including pike. Anything found can be brought into the classroom on site, which is fully equipped with microscopes and magnifiers, and the work produced can be taken back to school.

This is a unique site in a very busy part of central London. There has been very little vandalism or intrusion over the years, perhaps because local people helped to create the park and have grown up with it. Children can experience green wild spaces and walk through trees in a safe environment (14.2 and 14.3).

**Camley Street Natural Park, Late Summer**

A speckled wood butterfly, velvet brown,
wings spread out, lies sleepily on burdock,
its eyespots winking in the light.
Mint grows
in a watery bed.
Above its head
a dragonfly, blue brilliance,
jerks here and there.
Alders rise above the park, their branches
like brushes waving at the water life,
greeting the Coal and Fish Offices, sea of brick
sculpted curve moving gradually away.
Crack willow emeralds the grey.

Angela Inglis, 2007. (Courtesy of Rob Inglis)

## EARLY SKIRMISHES

During the 1980s, many of the historic buildings stood empty and unused, not only subject to neglect but increasingly vulnerable to accident, vandalism and arson.

The ten northern bays of the Eastern Coal Drops (ECD) were badly damaged by fire in 1985 (14.4). This part of the ECD was archaeologically the most interesting, having remained relatively unaltered from its original function, hence its Grade II listing, in contrast to the southern part, which had been adapted for warehouse use.

Fire in 1983 destroyed the interior of one of the buildings of the former Coal and Fish Offices and damaged another. The buildings were the subject of an application by National Carriers Limited to London Borough of Camden for demolition consent but NCL was frustrated by a concerted campaign by interested parties and in the press. The council rejected the application, and the case was heard in 1985 at a public enquiry where the heritage importance and potential for redevelopment persuaded the inspector to refuse the appeal. The building was not protected with a new roof until the late 1990s (14.5).

Some structures were patched up when they deteriorated, but others were clearly considered to fail the test. Notable among these, the surviving parts of the Potato Market were demolished by British Rail in 1988 (14.6) primarily to open the frontage onto York Way for commercial use.

## WAR IS DECLARED

British Rail (BR) was faced in the late 1980s with bringing the Channel Tunnel Rail Link (CTRL, now HS1) into London. Its planning options lay between an eastern route to Stratford, which was strongly supported by Michael Heseltine and Newham Council, and a largely tunnelled southern route through Clerkenwell to a low-level station underneath King's Cross. From a cost and engineering viewpoint, the eastern route was evidently preferable. But the situation was complicated by the government, which was not willing to subsidise the works for the CTRL or the termini BR intended to build. To pay for the terminus, BR was therefore determined to maximise its 'planning gain', the increase in value of the Railway Lands after obtaining development approval. Land at King's Cross was clearly far more valuable to corporate clients wishing to establish offices than land around the station at Stratford. BR was therefore strongly wedded to a King's Cross terminus.

BR's plans only became known to the public inadvertently, and exposed the fact that it planned to demolish 88 homes and 168 workplaces, affecting 326 residents and 1,620 local jobs. It had opened itself to comparison with promoters in the nineteenth century, bringing lines as far as the Euston Road through crowded 'slums'.

When the local community became aware of these plans local groups, comprising a mixed set of people from many backgrounds, formed the Railway Lands Community Development Group, later the King's Cross Railway Lands Group (KXRLG), championed by local Islington MP Chris Smith (now Lord Smith of Finsbury). The first public meeting in the Shaw Theatre on 17 September 1987 was packed.

Above left: **14.4**: Fire damage to the Eastern Coal Drops, viewed from the north, January 1988. (Malcolm Tucker)

Above right: **14.5**: The former Coal and Fish Offices from CSNP, January 2006. (Malcolm Tucker)

Right: **14.6**: Vestiges of the Potato Market after demolition, showing the cellars, January 1995. (Malcolm Tucker)

A key priority for the community was protecting the small local shops, which faced years of disruption. Such shopkeepers were often fatalistic in the face of 'the big people'.

## BLITZKRIEG

Realisation of this planning gain had to await completion of the railway works, which dictated the urgency with which BR pursued the King's Cross Railway Bill.

In June 1988, British Rail chose the London Regeneration Consortium (LRC), a partnership between the National Freight Corporation and Rosehaugh Stanhope, as developers of the 135 acres (55ha) of Railway Lands at King's Cross. LRC converted the 1850 Goods Offices into their headquarters and renamed the building Regeneration House: a portacabin outside was made into a permanent exhibition centre, first showing two competing master plans.

Soon after, Foster Associates were chosen as LRC's master planners. It was estimated about 30,000 jobs would be created, of which 90 per cent were in offices. Of these, only 8 per cent would go to local people. While 1,421 workers in eighty-nine firms would have to vacate the site, the developers were willing to invest £5 million in training schemes.

The Foster master plan, submitted in the revised outline planning application by LRC in October 1989, is shown in 14.7. Its main features were:

- two Manhattan style office 'spires', thirty-five and twenty-five storeys high marking the northern end of the site
- a 34 acre (14ha) oval park in the north
- a passenger concourse, triangular in plan, between King's Cross and St Pancras stations, requiring demolition of the Great Northern Hotel
- about 7 million sq. ft (650,000m$^2$) of office space, concentrated in the spires and to the east of the park, including streets built on a deck erected over the tracks leading north from King's Cross Station.

The LRC scheme underwent several substantial revisions after it was first submitted in 1988. Four years later the towers had grown to two forty-four-storey office blocks, but the office floor space had reduced to 5.25 million sq. ft (488,000m$^2$). Meanwhile the office market collapsed in 1990 and Rosehaugh declared insolvency some eighteen months later.

## WE SHALL FIGHT IN THE CLASSROOMS

The young people of Camden and Islington were invited to express, in the form of models, drawings and written work, their own ideas for the site, looking ahead a decade to its form after redevelopment. The King's Cross 2000 (KX2000) competition was organised by community activists, working with local schools and businesses, and was backed by the *Camden New Journal*. About 1,000 children participated.

**14.7**: Master plan submitted by LRC in the revised outline planning application, October 1989, Foster & Associates. (ICE)

A public exhibition of KX2000 entries was held from 9–20 November 1988 at St Pancras Chambers (formerly the Midland Grand Hotel). Entries (see examples in 14.8 and 14.9) were judged by an eminent panel that included the President of the Royal Institute of British Architects, writer Beryl Bainbridge and Godfrey Bradman, Chairman of Rosehaugh, part of the consortium. The exhibition was opened by Lord Jock Stallard, former St Pancras MP, who suggested Camden's planning department be brought there for 'a tutorial'.

While toilets appeared to be a preoccupation, housing was an area where the children's social conscience and passion came to the fore. One wrote:

Dear Sir, one of the teachers, her house is going to be knocked down. You should do something about it … It's very unfair and where is she going to live? The people might sign a petition to you and they might even write to the prime minister, they won't be pushed around. PS Think about it.

A scaled-down version of the KX2000 exhibition was part of the Civic Trust's stand for the 'Building a Better Britain' Exhibition held at the Islington Design Centre in April 1989. Prince Charles was much diverted by the stand (14.10).

## DAVID VERSUS GOLIATH

Membership of the King's Cross Railway Lands Group (KXRLG) numbered almost 400 local groups and individuals with a common concern for the King's Cross area and the Railway Lands site. Much of what it was seeking was affordable housing, training, community facilities, parks, jobs and a more cohesive, more balanced development between residential and offices. This proved very difficult despite some small successes.

The Railway Lands Group set up a series of workshops over 1988–91 that addressed themes of importance to the community. The first in November 1988 covered four days where LRC and Camden Council collaborated in a consultation with local people. It soon became apparent that one of the intentions was to destroy Camley Street Natural Park.

KXRLG also established an Economic Assessment Working Party with the help of University College London (UCL). In 1988 a *Social Audit* of the area was produced by Michael Edwards and Ellen Leopold of the Bartlett School at UCL. By working through various options of office space and housing units they concluded that a massive profit could still be made if less of the site were devoted to offices than to housing, perhaps 350,000m$^2$ compared with the 650,000m$^2$ proposed by LRC. To explain the computations to non-economists the KXRLG Working Party produced a pamphlet called *The King's Cross Development – People or Profit?* in July 1989, which was followed by a public meeting with the same title.

Further reports were commissioned from Michael Parkes, who had been engaged as a town planner. A summary report was prepared in November 1990, followed by *Towards a People's Plan* prepared by Michael Parkes and Daniel C. Mouawad with KXRLG. The professionalism and relevance of KXRLG's

**14.8**: King's Cross 2000: a typical master plan for the Railway Lands. (Marian Kamlish collection)

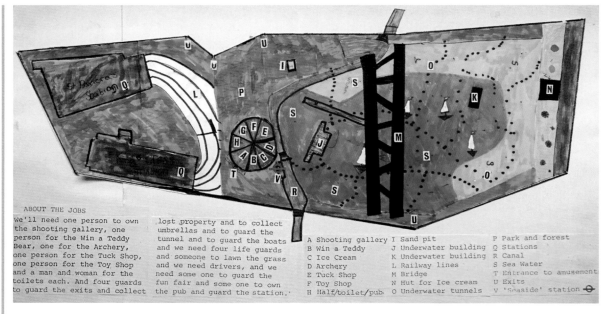

ABOUT THE JOBS

We'll need one person to own the shooting gallery, one person for the Win a Teddy Bear, one for the Archery, one person for the Tuck Shop, one person for the Toy Shop and a man and woman for the toilets each. And four guards to guard the exits and collect lost property and to collect umbrellas and to guard the tunnel and to guard the boats and we need four life guards and someone to lawn the grass and we need drivers, and we need some one to guard the fun fair and some one to own the pub and guard the station.

| | | |
|---|---|---|
| A Shooting gallery | I Sand pit | P Park and forest |
| B Win a Teddy | J Underwater building | Q Stations |
| C Ice Cream | K Underwater building | R Canal |
| D Archery | L Railway lines | S Sea Water |
| E Tuck Shop | M Bridge | T Entrance to amusement |
| F Toy Shop | N Hut for Ice cream | U Exits |
| H Half/toilet/pub | O Underwater tunnels | V 'Seaside' station |

**14.9**: King's Cross 2000: typical proposal details. (Marian Kamlish collection)

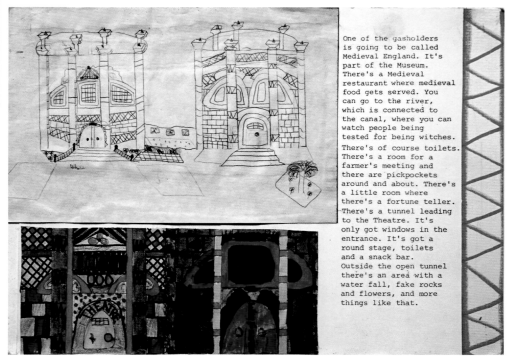

One of the gasholders is going to be called Medieval England. It's part of the Museum. There's a Medieval restaurant where medieval food gets served. You can go to the river, which is connected to the canal, where you can watch people being tested for being witches.
There's of course toilets. There's a room for a farmer's meeting and there are pickpockets around and about. There's a little room where there's a fortune teller. There's a tunnel leading to the Theatre. It's only got windows in the entrance. It's got a round stage, toilets and a snack bar.
Outside the open tunnel there's an area with a water fall, fake rocks and flowers, and more things like that.

work was recognised by a London Planning Achievement Award from the London Branch of the Royal Town Planning Institute.

Two alternative planning applications were submitted (one shown at 14.11) reflecting the community's priorities, with much more housing and retention of historic features including the Great Northern Hotel. The primary aim was to stop LRC getting planning permission for the Norman Foster plan.

The collapse of the property market, with the enormous over-supply of office space in London, and uncertainty over proposals for new rail works threatened a decade of blight. The group had long believed that a short- to medium-term initiative could help relieve the situation. It instructed Michael Parkes to look at short-term temporary uses, and Camden suggested the group develop the Interim Uses Initiative. This culminated in the report of December 1993, *Report on the Interim Uses for the King's Cross Railway Lands* prepared by Michael Parkes and Daniel C. Mouawad with KXRLG, which proposed immediate and longer-term actions that could be initiated without compromising permanent longer-term development.

## THE END OF THE BEGINNING

BR's King's Cross Railway Bill was deposited in Parliament in November 1988. Notices were issued regarding compulsory purchase and petitioning. The second reading was on 8 May 1989, sponsored by Sir George Young. In the debate, Chris Smith pointed out the difficulty the House would face as

**14.11**: King's Cross Railway Lands Group Scheme 1A. (KXRLG)

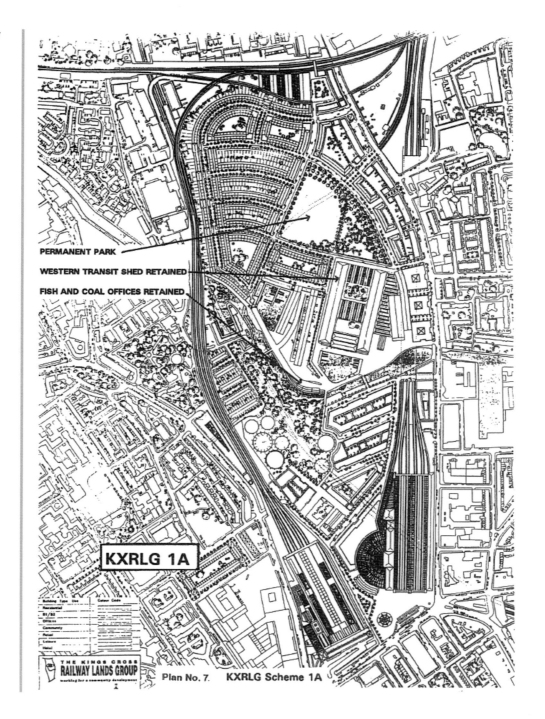

PERMANENT PARK

WESTERN TRANSIT SHED RETAINED

FISH AND COAL OFFICES RETAINED

KXRLG 1A

THE KINGS CROSS RAILWAY LANDS GROUP
working for a community development

Plan No. 7.    KXRLG Scheme 1A

BR had not yet planned or costed the line bringing trains to the station. He questioned the funding for the project. Northern MPs were strongly in support of the bill and it was voted through.

The wording of petitions had to follow elaborate and arcane formulae. KXRLG provided legal and other assistance to petitioners, guiding them in submitting 262 petitions against the bill to the House of Commons, a new record. MPs Chris Smith, Jeremy Corbyn, Tony Banks and Frank Dobson were on hand at the House to receive the petitions from Camden and Islington Councils and others. After BR had made numerous challenges to their legitimacy, another stage in the arcane process, 151 were allowed.

Neil Hamilton chaired the House of Commons Select Committee (SC). The fifty-one days of SC hearings were the longest since the Great Western Railway bill in 1834. Many petitioners spoke of losing homes and businesses, and the lack of compensation. The most serious problem was that station platforms were too short for the eighteen coach trains, a hook that BR tried to wriggle off, to the exasperation of the SC.

In the last few days, to the SC's surprise, BR came up with a plan for the line that involved extra tunnelling, causing costs to escalate by £1,900 million on top of the £830 million earlier cost estimate. The Department for Transport (DfT) then asked BR to examine and report on other options, opening the obvious alternative of an easterly approach and an overground station.

The SC finally reported on 26 June 1990. They decided that they had to approve the principle of the bill, but declared that they were only prepared to recommend proceeding with it on the basis that the Lords SC would satisfy itself regarding the route and obtain assurances on finance. It strongly criticised BR's conduct during the proceedings, pointing out that, at one critical stage, they had used lobbying that 'verged on being a contempt of Parliament'.

BR's recommendations for the eastern route were not made until autumn 1991. They had persisted with a low-level station at King's Cross rather than an overground solution.

The third reading debate was held on 28 January 1992. Chris Smith attacked the funding, but the bill was approved by 165 to 5 for passing on to the Lords.

The Economic Assessment Working Party now produced a detailed report: *King's Cross Project – costs and financial viability*. The report showed the extent of the funding BR needed. It was sent to BR, DfT and *The Times*. KXRLG was thanked by the Treasury for an interesting and helpful paper.

The second reading in the Lords was on 1 June 1992. Lord Greenhill was chair of the Lords Committee, which held seventeen days of hearings. Cast iron guarantees were demanded from the promoters and the government on funding.

The Lords Committee reported in July 1992, stating that they had 'weighed the advantages the bill would bring against the savage local impacts of the scheme in human and material terms during construction'. They accepted the petitioners' argument that it would be wrong to pass the bill 'if we were not satisfied that the powers it bestowed would be used'. They suggested the minister 'make a statement of intent during the Third Reading of the bill'.

KXRLG could show that 'no undertakings or statements have been made to BR in relation to funding these projects in 1995/96'. Further reports were produced by various bodies, and in March 1993 the government announced two alternatives: one a tunnelled route from Stratford to the proposed King's Cross low-level station for which BR was seeking powers; the other a tunnel from Stratford to Mildmay

Grove near Canonbury, from where it would run along the route of the North London Line to York Way before swinging south to St Pancras.

On 24 January 1994 John MacGregor, Secretary of State for Transport, announced that St Pancras had been chosen as the terminal and British Rail had been instructed to withdraw the King's Cross Railway Bill. This signalled the start of the battle for the Caledonian Road.

## THE BATTLE FOR THE CALEDONIAN ROAD

While the decision to make St Pancras the CTRL terminal was finally a triumph of good sense – it was on the surface and making use of an under-used station – millions of pounds had been wasted in abortive planning.

But further conflict lay ahead. Union Railways, acting for the government, proposed to put the rail link in a tunnel below most of Islington, surfacing just west of the Caledonian Road. The tunnel would be constructed by 'cut and cover' across the road, entailing up to five years' closure, with immense disruption to the area and no compensation to shopkeepers for loss of trade either during construction or later. Although the 'safeguarding' map published in early 1994 showed no homes would be demolished, the area was immediately blighted. Cally Traders Group and Cally Rail Group were promptly formed to promote better solutions and mitigate the effects on the area.

14.12: Islington Council poster campaign, 1993. (ILHC)

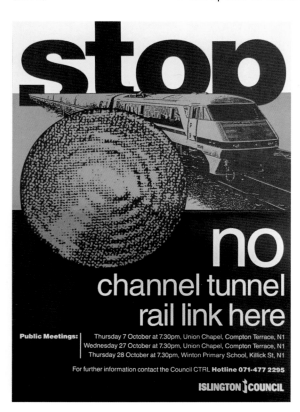

Islington Council supported the community affected but had to mediate between those opposed to the new route and those concentrating on getting it into tunnel (14.12). Two alternatives were proposed by engineering consultants engaged by Islington Council: one in tunnel, resurfacing in the Railway Lands, the other a partly tunnelled option, surfacing on the railway bank behind Gifford Street. These were ignored by the promoters.

The Channel Tunnel Rail Link Bill received its first reading in November 1994. Supported by the council, Cally Rail Group and Cally Traders ensured that 230 local residents and businesses petitioned against the bill, more than any other area along the route. In summer 1995 the SC, after hearing evidence, clearly favoured a tunnelled option but government opposition led to the committee receiving two new schemes to consider: one fully tunnelled, the other, promoted by Union Railways, surfacing next to the East Coast Main Line. The second received consent, and the CTRL Bill became law in December 1996.

LCR were given the contract to build the link, but hit a financial crisis in 1998, leading to a £6 billion bail-out with public money. The link was divided into Stages 1 and 2, the second stage being from Ebbsfleet to St Pancras via Stratford.

Facilitating works in the Caledonian Road were finally started in 2002 with the strengthening of sewers and water mains. Thanks to a special compensation scheme, hard won by Cally Traders and Cally Rail Group, local traders could claim for loss of trade. The CTRL bridge across the East Coast Main Line was launched over Christmas 2003. The tunnels under the Caledonian Road were bored in early 2004. Following a public enquiry in January 2004, the Planning Inspector turned down CTRL's application to work 24/7 for the next three years.

York Way was closed for three months from January 2005 as the viaduct was demolished and the road rerouted to allow CTRL to run a bridge over it. This created the Islington Triangle site from land between the ECML and York Way that had previously been a fan of goods and mineral sidings.

## THE BEGINNING OF THE END

Argent St George were appointed developers of King's Cross Railway Lands in 2000.

In July 2001, Argent St George published *Principles for a Human City* with more than 3,000 copies distributed. It referred to the King's Cross Railway Lands as King's Cross Central. In October 2002, Argent St George published *A Framework for Regeneration*, a consultation document of which more than 10,000 copies were distributed in Camden and Islington.

In May 2004, Argent St George submitted the first outline planning application for King's Cross Central, applying for 486,000m$^2$ of the available 720,000m$^2$ of built-up area to be office space, leaving 32.5 per cent of space available for residential uses and community facilities. The fourteen-week public consultation began in June and ended in September.

A revised outline planning application was submitted the following year, which Camden Council provisionally agreed in March 2006, despite many objections, and consented in November. Opposing groups formed the King's Cross – Think Again campaign which took Camden to judicial review in the High Court in May 2007, but lost the case.

# fifteen

# Transition and Regeneration

## SMALL BUSINESS COLONIES

15.1: Scenesetters Ltd: colonising the Coal Drops with craft enterprises, 1984. (Richard Holmes)

The Interim Use Initiative (see last chapter) needed little stimulus. Artists and craftspeople are forever seeking studios that they can afford and were naturally attracted to derelict or neglected Victorian warehouses and arches, with their sense of abandoned history and cavernous spaces.

Some historical buildings were colonised more formally through rental, for example the coal drops and the arches under Wharf Road, others by squatting such as in the stables opposite the Culross Building that ran from Battle Bridge Road to Goods Way. Photographers used these stables for exhibitions, antique restorers as woodworking studios, and a violin maker to repair violins, with a sideline in restoring Mercedes cars.

The coal drops from the early 1980s housed a variety of businesses, including the famous Bagley's nightclub. Neighbours included workshops that made scenery for the theatre (15.1). John Sullivan, who made barrows and repaired them, had been in the stable arches since 1982, having moved from Covent Garden when that area was redeveloped. Richard Aumonier was a sculptor involved with restoration of classical buildings. He found the arches offered not only peace and quiet (when not reverberating with music from the clubs) but also a space where he could create noise and dust. Another craftsman carved polystyrene into lettering.

The large-scale dereliction of the Railway Lands created its own opportunities. In December 1994 the former Train Assembly Shed area became home to the Raceway, the UK's longest indoor go-karting circuit with 1,050m of track. Some of the former coal stacking ground on the western side of York Way was, through the 1990s, central London's only full-length golf driving range.

## RAVE SCENE

The Motor Repair Depot, by then known as the Roadline Depot, was entered by turning left at the walled end of Battle Bridge Road, opposite the former Mission Hall of the Culross Building. Owned by National Carriers Ltd, it had fallen into disuse by the mid-1980s. The large repair sheds and earlier buildings, together with an assortment of equipment and vehicles, were abandoned. Culross residents and other magpies would pick over the remains, amazed that the site could be left empty and unsecured for so long.

The depot sheds and warehouses proved an ideal location to squat for the Mutoid Waste Company, which moved there in the late 1980s from the old bus station in the Caledonian Road. Influenced by the film *Mad Max* they became famous for building giant welded post-apocalyptic sculptures from scrap machinery and waste materials and for customising broken down cars. They developed a good relationship with many Culross residents. As one recalls, 'I gave them my car and they turned it into a crocodile' (Steve Neylon, interviewed by Giles Rollastone for *King's Cross Voices*).

Embracing the burgeoning acid house movement by the late 1980s, despite their philosophy of creativity without artificial stimulants, they organised large shed parties, decorating the depot with large murals, mutated cars, machines, sculptures made from waste material and dragons belching flames. Charging a tenner entry, within two weeks they were overwhelmed by numbers. Some semblance of legality was maintained by inviting the police, showing them around and creating a favourable impression, but the police evicted them in 1989 after several raids. By then a collective of some twenty artists had been together for five years.

**15.2**: Mutoid Waste Company at the 100 Club, Ivan Tarashenko on right. (Steve Payne)

They returned briefly to squat the buildings for a memorial event for their drummer Ivan Tarashenko who had been killed in the 1987 King's Cross Underground fire. In his memory, 400 people played drums on various objects including cars and dustbins. The noise was indescribable …

Another Culross resident described the experience as, 'Mad Max gone mad! It was absolutely incredible and you just felt like you were living at the centre of the Universe' (Abigail Dodd, interviewed by Giles Rollastone for *King's Cross Voices*).

Some twenty-five years after these events, Mutoid Waste and their recycled steampunk creations feature regularly at Glastonbury. Joe Rush, one of the two founders, designed and directed the vehicles and special effects for the spectacular closing ceremony of the London 2012 Paralympic Games, and the mobile stages on which Coldplay and Rihanna performed so memorably.

## BAR AND NIGHTCLUB SCENE

15.3: TDK at The Cross, with the Coal and Fish Offices illuminated, in August 2006. The nightclub venue was in the old stables, in the arches under Wharf Road. (Fabio Venni)

King's Cross goods yard had always operated twenty-four hours a day, but this activity took place out of the gaze of the public. After the Criminal Justice Act of 1994 had curtailed large outdoor raves, King's Cross once more came alive at night, this time with young people going to clubs that opened at midnight through until the morning. Clubbers flocked to the abandoned Victorian warehouses and brick railway arches at King's Cross for the legendary warehouse parties. Younger people, turning off Wharf Road that joined York Way north of the canal, knew the area as 'Club City'.

Bagley's was the nightclub that started and underpinned the area's nightlife for fifteen to twenty years. It occupied the warehouse at the southern end of the Eastern Coal Drops and four arches under

Wharf Road. The owners, Johnny and Billy Reilly, invested heavily in soundproofing and engaged with the residential community to respond to the inevitable complaints. These could be many and varied: Camley Street Natural Park was concerned that the rhythmic thumping was disturbing the mating habits of amphibians.

Bagley's, which later became Canvas, hosted several clubs on a regular basis, one such being TDK (15.3). Another was The Church, initially a gathering point for Aussies but increasingly attracting Londoners, which became infamous for antipodean high jinks and drunken revelry, including strippers, on a Sunday afternoon. Its motto was: 'If you haven't sinned, you can't be forgiven.'

The spaces that were once filled with revellers finally fell silent during Christmas 2007, when The Cross, The Key and Canvas were shut, leaving London bereft of the semi-derelict quarter that fostered some of the finest warehouse parties in the capital since the mid-1980s.

# DEMOLITION

Angela Inglis' photographic exploration ('Railway Lands', 2007) was driven by the history attached to the land and her photographer's eye for the changing light intensity that played over the historical fabric. Central to the landscapes at King's Cross were the gasholders with their fretted framework.

### THE GASHOLDERS – King's Cross

I often wandered past to see your wheels
of steel intricately wrought like lace stained pink,
held by annulets, lovers' rings with black
square stones. At evening I watched the sun splash
your pink with red, and conjure your hoops to join,
circling chains twining and intertwining
like dancers in the air. White vapours skimmed
behind your capitals, then disappeared
to leave deep blue sharpening your silhouette.

Angela Inglis, 2007. (Extract, courtesy of Rob Inglis)

15.4: Last of the Triplets, January 2002, Angela Inglis. (Courtesy of Rob Inglis)

15.5: The dismantling of Gasholder 8, March 2011. (Argent)

15.6: Demolition of Culross Building, July 2008, woodcut. (Marianne Fox-Ockinga)

Their loss was very deeply felt by many. Most were dismantled in 2001 to make way for the CTRL, the guide frames and lattice girders of the listed Siamese Triplets (15.4) being stored for reuse.

Gasholder 8 was similarly dismantled in 2011 (15.5) and placed in storage before being refurbished. Between their circumferential lattice girders, the cast-iron columns of the guide frames were formed of two or three segments with secret bolted fixings internally, suggesting that assembly had required lithe young people to be lowered into the column. These joints, now strapped, can just be seen in the relocated Gasholder 8 (16.14, page 198).

One of three Stanley Buildings was also demolished for the CTRL, and ten years later one of the two remaining buildings was demolished ahead of the creation of Pancras Square.

Marianne Fox-Ockinga, with the help of residents and contractors, established her artist's easel on the roof of the Culross Building and on other vantage points, recording the demolition all around until the wrecking ball forced such locations to be abandoned. The Culross Buildings were demolished in July–August 2008 to make way for King's Cross Boulevard, which became the north–south axis (15.6).

## CONSTRUCTION OF CTRL

The CTRL was the country's first major railway project for over 100 years. Section 2 from Ebbsfleet to St Pancras was started in mid-2001 and opened in November 2007.

At King's Cross/St Pancras the major work involved:

*   the demolition works referred to above
*   refurbishment of the Barlow Shed
*   construction of an extension shed with six central international platforms for 400m-long Eurostar trains, three platforms for CTRL domestic trains and four platforms for Midland mainline trains
*   underground works, including two new ticket halls
*   track layout from the tunnel portal between Caledonian Road and York Way across the Railway Lands into St Pancras.

The progress of construction in 2005 can be seen from the satellite image (15.7), and the completed station in 2010 from another satellite image (15.8).

## START OF KING'S CROSS CENTRAL WORKS

Work on King's Cross Central got underway in late 2006 with land clearance and site investigation but major construction did not start for several years, although some work continued through the financial crisis of 2008.

An associated task was the completion of the new King's Cross Station concourse ahead of the 2012 London Olympics. Preparatory works can be seen in 15.8. This replaced the 1970s concourse

**15.7**: The construction of CTRL, September 2005. (Map data: Google, Digital Globe)

**15.8**: Early works in the Railway Lands, June 2010. (Map data: Google, Bluesky)

at the front of King's Cross Station, allowing the creation of the new station forecourt. In the goods yard, the Western Goods Shed had not yet been demolished, but early work on the Granary and Transit Sheds was underway.

**15.9**: The construction of King's Cross Central, April 2017. (Map data: Google)

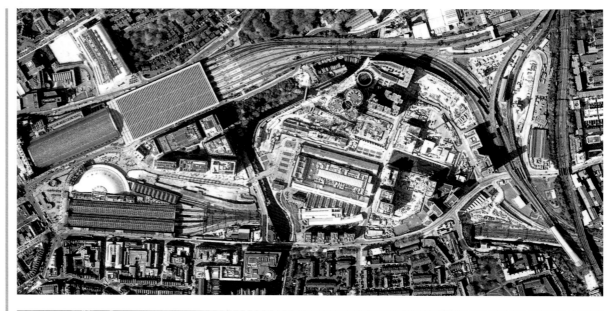

**15.10**: Central St Martins' new home, the former Train Assembly Shed, undergoing redevelopment. (Argent)

**15.11**: Quentin Blake's wrap of the surviving Stanley Building, 2007. His involvement in King's Cross has been strengthened through the House of Illustration in the Eastern Transit Shed. (Argent)

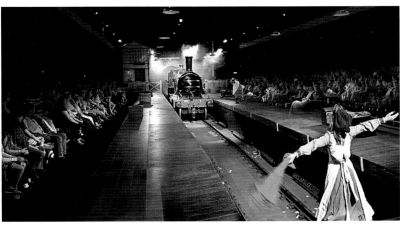

**15.12**: *The Railway Children*: Bobbie averting disaster by stopping a real steam locomotive, King's Cross Theatre.

**15.13**: The Pond Club in Lewis Cubitt Park provided an unusual swimming experience amid the rising tower blocks, 2016. (Argent)

**15.14**: Circus of Light in Granary Square, part of 'Lumière London' (14–17 January 2016), when King's Cross was transformed into an illuminated festival of light, music and art. (Argent)

Major building works were undertaken over the five years up to 2017, an April 2017 satellite image confirming the progress (15.9). The Central St Martins complex was completed as was Gasholder Park, the Midland Goods Shed and areas under the Handyside Canopies. Work on the residential buildings within the Siamese Triplet gasholder frames was almost complete, and Coal Drops Yard was well under way for a scheduled 2018 completion.

## A CATALYST FOR CHANGE

The redevelopment of the Granary, the Train Assembly Shed and the Transit Sheds created an immense complex on six floors (15.10). Coming at the start of the King's Cross Central project, the tenancy of this set of buildings would be a catalyst and set the context for what followed. The choice of Central St Martins was inspired, and placed creativity, energy and vitality at the heart of the King's Cross Central development. This centre of excellence combines design, research, academia and business with galleries and theatre to demonstrate students' work.

## SPECTACLE AS ATTRACTION

A wide variety of spectacle has been used to attract people to King's Cross Central through recreating history, through theatre, music, sports and play. While Granary Square is the main venue, events have been held also in Lewis Cubitt Square, under the West Handyside Canopy, and in the Granary atrium, known as the Crossing. These have helped to make King's Cross Central an important leisure destination and a centre for food and entertainment. Examples are given in 15.11 to 15.15.

## NAMING OF STREETS

King's Cross Central is creating a new locality with office and residential buildings, public squares, streets and parks. This has provided an opportunity to give the streets and public spaces names that resonate locally, names associated with people, objects and events that have helped shape King's Cross.

A public consultation was launched in March 2013 that provoked a response locally, nationally and internationally from over 5,000 entrants submitting over 10,000 entries. Filtering these involved an assessment of who and what had made King's Cross, with an emphasis on interest and engagement rather than weight of numbers behind the entry.

Entries were divided into thirty-five themes and then into six categories for assessment: site history, local area, local people, rail industry, station history and nightlife. These were then assessed against the seven criteria that had served well up until then:

- length of time connected to King's Cross
- existing references
- proximity to King's Cross
- direct connection to King's Cross
- historical impact
- impact on King's Cross Station
- legacy

A total of thirty-eight names made it onto the preliminary shortlist, which was then submitted to the London Borough of Camden, Royal Mail and the emergency services, which each has its own criteria for street names, for approval. This resulted in a final shortlist of thirty names, creating a pool that can be drawn on for naming.

The first name to be chosen from the pool was Wollstonecraft Street, after Mary Wollstonecraft, a nineteenth-century writer, philosopher and advocate for women's rights, as well as mother of Mary Shelley, author of *Frankenstein*. She is buried in the graveyard of St Pancras Old Church.

A second name has recently been adopted: Bagley Walk. Bagley reflects both the industrial heritage, Joseph Bagley & Co. of Knottingley, West Yorkshire, who were glass bottle manufacturers, and the nightclub scene described earlier.

## PANORAMA

The view taken from 5 Pancras Square (15.16), the new offices of the London Borough of Camden, shows the extent of works completed and underway in the former Railway Lands north of the Regent's Canal in 2015.

On the left, Gasholder No. 8 had been erected, but the black frame does not show up well against Tapestry Apartments. Tower cranes were working on the Siamese Triplet gasholders and the foundations of buildings to be erected inside the gasholder frames. On this side the Western and Eastern Coal Drops were awaiting approval of Heatherwick's plans for Coal Drops Yard. Beyond the coal drops, Lewis Cubitt Square and Lewis Cubitt Park had been laid out, and construction of new office blocks around these open spaces was underway.

The dramatic right-angle turn of the canal imbues the Coal and Fish Offices, on which restoration work has yet to start, with their special character. The other side of Granary Square, the restored Granary grandly imposes its new identity as the University of the Arts. To the east of Granary Square, the Lighterman Restaurant was near completion. Flanking the Eastern Transit Shed is Regeneration House, one of the first historic buildings restored. On its eastern side, work was underway to convert the Midland Shed and Eastern Handyside Canopy into a new supermarket.

**15.15**: PUNKX celebrated the experimental and creative scene that grew up at King's Cross in the 1980s to 1990s. Joe Rush of Mutoid Waste Company, looking slightly incongruous, in Granary Square, June 2016. (Argent)

**15.16**: Panorama, 2015. (Argent)

THE KING'S CROSS STORY: 200 YEARS OF HISTORY IN THE RAILWAY LANDS

# A Sunday Stroll up King's Boulevard

# sixteen

## PLAN OF RAILWAY LANDS

Some 180 years after the walk undertaken in Chapter 1, we shall take a stroll around the transformed Railway Lands, noting particularly how the historic features have been adapted for the development of King's Cross Central and how the new buildings complement the historic features.

The route we will take through King's Cross Central, starting at the station, is shown in 16.1.

**16.1**: A walk through King's Cross Central. (Based on Argent plan)

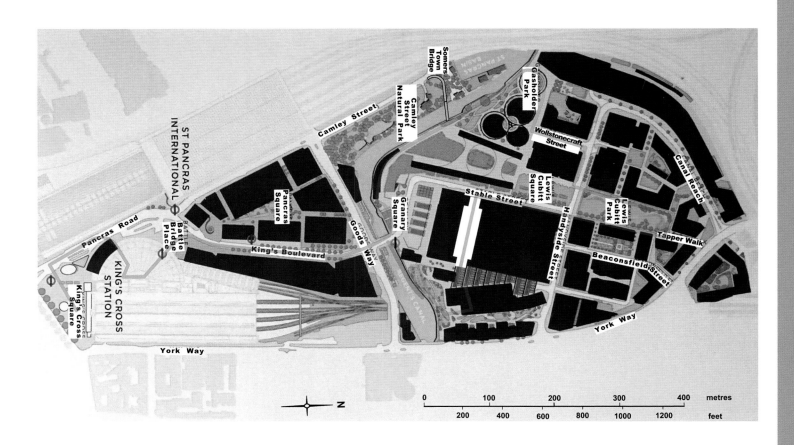

# KING'S CROSS STATION AND GREAT NORTHERN HOTEL

King's Cross/St Pancras with its international, main line, suburban and six underground railway lines is the most connected transport hub in Europe. The cluster of buildings in front of the station have all been removed, exposing the original façade (16.2). Light now pours in through the glazed roofs into the twin sheds, brilliantly revealed from the square. Our starting point will be King's Cross Square at the front of King's Cross Station.

**16.2**: The front of the Passenger Station viewed across King's Cross Square. (Argent)

Moving along the front in a westerly direction, we meet the curve of the Great Northern Hotel. Its concave front faces the western façade of the station it served, the space now bridged by the new concourse. But we follow the convex side facing St Pancras Station (16.3), past the taxi ranks, before turning around the northern end to enter the departure side of the station under the new concourse.

The roof rises like a multi-stemmed tree that spreads into a canopy of intersecting branches, creating space and light on the departures side with little need for supporting columns. Keeping the space clear of the ubiquitous London pigeon is a job for a feathery professional – and its handler! (16.4)

We take the opportunity to appreciate the statue of Sir Nigel Gresley on the west wall of the station (16.5) and, avoiding the throng with cameras trained on Platform 9¾, exit the station to Battle Bridge Place.

**16.3**: The Great Northern Hotel facing St Pancras Station. (Argent)

A SUNDAY STROLL UP KING'S BOULEVARD

**16.4**: The new departures concourse at King's Cross Station. (Getty)

**16.5**: Sir Nigel Gresley. (Matt Brown, *Londonist*)

THE KING'S CROSS STORY: 200 YEARS OF HISTORY IN THE RAILWAY LANDS

# BATTLE BRIDGE PLACE TO GRANARY SQUARE

Battle Bridge Place (16.6), just like King's Cross Square, is a public meeting space and transit area that serves the King's Cross/St Pancras complex, St Pancras Station notably lacking such outside spaces.

The German Gymnasium is now gloriously restored and has been converted into a restaurant. We pass through the generous area of outside seating to enter the large ground-floor bar and dining area, and admire the form before ascending one of the two sweeping staircases to the dining area occupying part of the gallery that formerly extended around the building (3.13, page 49), now lined with *tables à deux* and banquettes (16.7). Here we can appreciate the timber ribs that support the roof. These are composed of twelve laminated layers of timber bolted together. This was the roof form initially used by Lewis Cubitt for the King's Cross train sheds. There are hooks in the beams to which climbing ropes were attached for gymnastics.

**16.6**: Battle Bridge Place with (from left): German Gymnasium, King's Boulevard, Google Building and Western Concourse. (Argent)

**16.7**: The interior of the German Gymnasium, showing ribs and roof timbers. (Argent)

As part of the conversion, tie bars have been inserted at each timber rib to restrict any movement of the external wall under the new loading.

Exiting the German Gymnasium, we can observe the one remaining Stanley Building on the north side, now restored as offices, before continuing up King's Boulevard. The east side of the street from Battle Bridge Place to Goods Way is the location of the new Google UK Headquarters Building, which promises to be a remarkable example of modern architecture. Offices also line the west side of the street.

The Google Building will not be described here, but for the general public, the most interesting feature will be the roof (16.8) with its views over the King's Cross train sheds and the tracks leading to Gasworks Tunnel, which so narrowly avoided being concreted over for more offices.

Further west, a cluster of new office buildings surround Pancras Square. These include new offices and a leisure centre for the London Borough of Camden, the Council Offices affording a magnificent panoramic view over the HS1 approaches to St Pancras and the new architecture springing up to the north (16.9). It shows our route over King's Bridge into Granary Square, past a tiered terrace overlooking Regent's Canal that has become a favourite area for al fresco snacks.

**16.8**: The roof of the Google Building. (Argent)

**16.9**: A panoramic view over Granary Square. (Argent)

**16.10**: The view south to King's Boulevard from Granary Square over the former Granary Basin. (Argent)

THE KING'S CROSS STORY: 200 YEARS OF HISTORY IN THE RAILWAY LANDS

Granary Square has made a feature of the embedded rails, capstans and turntables by varied use of paving. Regrettably this does not extend to a clear delineation of the former Granary Basin, a forgotten historical feature that the arrays of fountains do little to recall for the public's comprehension (16.10).

## GRANARY SQUARE TO COAL DROPS YARD

From Granary Square to Coal Drops Yard we can take either the high road, the canal corniche, or the low road, both seen in the photo impression (16.11). The low road leads past former stables arches and nightclub venues. The high road, formerly Wharf Road but now renamed Bagley Walk, goes past the former Coal and Fish Offices and continues alongside the canal over the former stables arches, with raised beds and planters on both sides.

At the time of writing, Coal Drops Yard was under construction and is scheduled to open in 2018. The approved scheme by Thomas Heatherwick includes a striking modification to the roofscape (16.12). Both Western and Eastern Coal Drops roofs are being swept inwards and upwards to meet in an apex above a new bridge spanning the yard. This will provide an extra floor with a glazed gallery

**16.11**: Coal and Fish Offices with high road and low road to Coal Drops Yard. (Argent)

**16.12**: Coal Drops Yard, an extract from Design and Access Statement. (Heatherwick)

overlooking Coal Drops Yard. The upper floor levels are being lowered to the level of the viaducts and bridge link over much of the lengths of the two ranges, which will simplify access for the disabled.

The combination of Victorian brickwork and modern architecture will prove stunning, but some elements of its justification have been contentious. The southern ends will be left relatively little altered, but it is the fire-damaged north end of the Eastern Coal Drops that is archaeologically the most interesting part, and much historical detail will be lost here. Another loss will be the magnificent expanse of blue granite setts in the yard, all but fragments being replaced by precisely laid new setts, to satisfy the needs for disabled access. The open arches will be infilled with plate glass shopfronts.

THE KING'S CROSS STORY: 200 YEARS OF HISTORY IN THE RAILWAY LANDS

## TO GASHOLDER PARK

From Coal Drops Yard we return to Bagley Walk, and pass Somers Town Bridge, a pedestrian footbridge completed in summer 2017 that crosses the canal and drops down into Camley Street (16.13). We pass the Siamese Triplet gasholders, ably preserved, but at the expense of their dignity and the power of their silhouettes, by being filled with prime residential property.

It is but a few more yards to Gasholder 8, its guide frames, guide wheels and lattice girders beautifully restored and allowed to stand in an open space for the enjoyment of visitors, who are protected from the elements by a striking modern shelter that encircles the central space (16.14 and 16.15).

**16.13**: Bagley's Walk as it approaches Gasholder Park, with the Siamese Triplets on the right. Somers Town Bridge is in the left foreground, with St Pancras Water Point on the far left. (Peter Darley)

**16.14**: Gasholder Park.
(Argent)

## LEWIS CUBITT PARK AND SQUARE

Once we leave Gasholder Park, our route takes us east past the Plimsoll Building, before we turn north into Wollstonecraft Street and east into Handyside Street. This leads along the south side of Lewis Cubitt Park, the largest area of green public space. As in other landscaped areas, careful thought has gone into the plantings, and we take Lewis Cubitt Walk around the park admiring the paperbark maples and other selected trees (16.16). The Pond Club shown in 15.13 on page 183 was always a temporary feature and has now disappeared.

The view in 16.16 shows us a world of new office architecture taking shape, with the cores of major buildings rising on the left of the picture. Beyond these the 580ft (177m) long Western Transit Shed is prominent, on what is now Stable Street. Work had evidently not yet started on Coal Drops Yard, although this was nearing completion in early 2018. Lewis Cubitt Square is seen to be hosting an event. We head south along first the east arm of Lewis Cubitt Walk and then Stable Street.

**16.15**: Detail of Gasholder 8. Note St Pancras Water Point and Francis Crick Institute beyond, October 2017. (Peter Darley)

**16.16**: Lewis Cubitt Park and Square. (Argent)

## STABLE STREET AND WESTERN TRANSIT SHED

On our left, the walls of the Western Transit Shed still stand, and are 25ft high in a single storey. Their huge doorways remain to define the spaces, which have now been converted into offices with shops and restaurants at street level. Little remains of the wrought-iron roof trusses and cast-iron arcades, but one section of roof survives above an office at first floor level.

    The historic fabric has been admirably exposed in Dishoom Restaurant (16.17), not only successfully adapting the space but enhancing it on three levels, including the former stables in the basement.

**16.17**: Dishoom Restaurant and Western Transit Shed: the bar and entrance on ground floor. (Argent)

Just before Dishoom, at 11 Stable Street, is the Visitor Centre for the new development. Beyond Dishoom, we enter one of the doorways of the Western Transit Shed that creates a passage across the former goods sheds, connecting Stable Street to the West Handyside Canopy. Passing the stairs to Argent's offices at first floor level in the Western Transit Shed we enter the large atrium at the rear of the Granary.

## GRANARY AND TRAIN ASSEMBLY SHED

Off the atrium is the entrance to Central St Martins (CSM), which occupies the buildings that were formerly the Granary, the Train Assembly Shed and the Eastern Transit Shed. Looking towards the rear of the Granary from the entrance to CSM, the outlines of the four bays that made up the Train Assembly Shed (see 4.7, page 57) are dramatically revealed by scars on the north wall, as shown in the panorama below (16.18). The western bay, seen here on the right, had offices built in 1897–99 on the first floor, the scar of which is also visible. The electric lift shaft was carved out of the north wall in 1926.

The atrium, known as the Crossing, provides a space for exhibiting not unlike the Turbine Hall at Tate Modern. When no events are on, the Crossing resounds to the staccato striking of ping-pong balls as people enjoy the free tables provided.

**16.18**: A view of the north wall of the Granary. (Peter Darley)

## HANDYSIDE CANOPIES AND MIDLAND SHED

Emerging from the Granary atrium we enter another covered space used for markets, exhibitions and other events: the West Handyside Canopy (16.19). The canopy spans from the Eastern Transit Shed to the Midland Goods Shed, flanked on the south side by Regeneration House, the former Goods Offices, now with a café and seating under the canopy.

Crossing to the Midland Goods Shed we enter Waitrose supermarket, which occupies both the Midland Goods Shed and the East Handyside Canopy. Here we observe the spandrel beams of the west arcade of the departure side roof of the 1850 Temporary Passenger Station (16.20), the only original elements of the station that have witnessed both the arrival of Queen Victoria and more than a century of trading in the humble potato.

## REGENT'S CANAL FRONTAGE

We leave the supermarket by its main entrance facing the canal, seen illuminated on the right in 16.21. Turning right we take the path along the front of the Midland Goods Shed and Regeneration House. This brings us to the Eastern Transit Shed offices that front Granary Square and now incorporate the

House of Illustration. Founded by Sir Quentin Blake, it opened in July 2014, a charitable trust dedicated to book illustration and the graphic arts.

We turn the corner into Granary Square, noting the lines of railway tracks and turntables picked out by variations in paving. Facing the Eastern Transit Shed Offices, we note a difference in the tone of brick on the façade of the building, the result of rebuilding following the November 1940 bomb (12.1, page 143). Shrapnel damage can still be seen on the adjoining side of the Granary.

From here we turn east and, with the massing of King's Place as a backdrop, descend to the towpath where we encounter Word on the Water, the London Bookbarge (16.22), a 1920s Dutch barge converted to a floating bookshop. It is an appropriate and relaxing place to pause and reflect on the intensity of human endeavour that is springing up all around, embracing architecture, media, the arts, biotechnology, IT and food and entertainment.

**16.21**: A panorama along Regent's Canal, looking west. (Argent)

**16.22**: Word on the Water, the London Bookbarge, with the glazed bulk of King's Place in the middle distance, October 2017. (Peter Darley)

# Epilogue

Looking back, the demolition of the Euston Arch appeared to have been forgotten as British Rail, only a generation later, planned a similar fate for the Great Northern Hotel together with a Canary Wharf style office city at King's Cross. Modernisation of our railways would once again require the sacrifice of their Victorian heritage.

With so many opportunities for things to go wrong from the 1980s to the present, how have we avoided these destinies and arrived at such a good place? That we are now able to enjoy and appreciate the Victorian heritage is a notable success for the developers, and it is right that they should get the credit. But let us not forget the protracted battles that were fought over two decades by the local community and its champions, and what might have been the outcome had their efforts not combined with economic serendipity.

If, as Frank Dobson so succinctly advised the HS2 Select Committee, 'the community has all the common sense that promoters lack', a sentiment that most will share, how can we harness its needs and wishes more effectively to the decision-making process in order to work towards better outcomes in the future? The community understands more profoundly than developers how the present can and should be enriched by the past.

When faced with the challenges of major urban redevelopment it is fair to say that the visions of promoters and the community do not appear to be converging. More than ever we must ask ourselves what kind of city we want to live in, and that is not a question this book has even attempted to answer.

Although the combination of new and old may not please everyone, and the costs were very high, the transformation of King's Cross and St Pancras has broadcast how the industrial past should be respected and celebrated, a message that has transmitted up to the key heritage features on the northern bank of the Regent's Canal.

We experience a range of powerful emotions when we enter the refurbished Barlow Shed at St Pancras, foremost among them a sense of pride. We have similar feelings when we face the Passenger Station from King's Cross Square, before entering the spectacular new departures concourse, grafted so dramatically onto the west wall of the 1852 terminus and onto the crescent of the 1854 Great Northern Hotel. We can already celebrate the successful transformation of the 1852 Granary complex and the process of regeneration that is transforming other historical features.

At King's Cross, our past appears secure and our future will, as a result, be immeasurably enriched.

The Gasholder Triplets in 1997, taken from Goods Way, Angela Inglis. (Courtesy of Rob Inglis)

# Purchasing Power of the Pound, 1817 to 2017

Comparing the prices of wages, salaries, contracts and other monetized values during the last 200 years can be difficult without at least some idea of how inflation (or deflation) in prices has affected the purchasing power of the pound.

No such comparison can be anything more than very approximate. Expenditure patterns changed drastically over the period, as also did the quality of goods, and the method of determining the price index.

**A1.1**: Retail prices index and relative purchasing power of pound, 1820 to 1917.

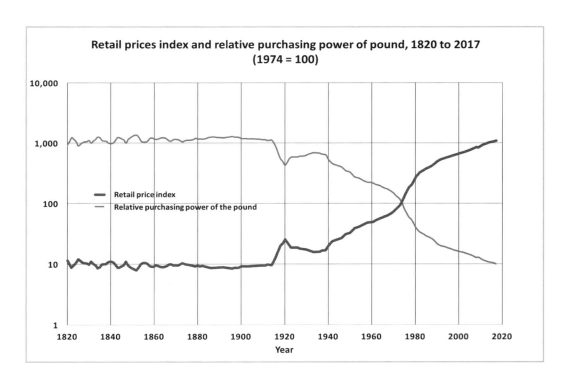

**Retail prices index and relative purchasing power of pound, 1820 to 2017 (1974 = 100)**

The sources of the price indices are:

| | |
|---|---|
| To 1850 | E.H. Phelps-Brown and S. Hopkins, 'Seven Centuries of the Prices of Consumables compared with Builders' Wage-rates', *Economica*, Nov. 1956, pp.296–314. |
| 1850–70 | W. Layton and G. Crowther, *An Introduction to the Study of Prices,* 1935, Table 1. |
| 1870–1947 | C.H. Feinstein, *National Income, Expenditure and Output of the United Kingdom 1855– 1965,* 1972, Tables 24 and 25. |
| 1947–2017 | The all-items RPI as published monthly by the Office for National Statistics. |

The chart plots the retail price index and the relative purchasing power of the pound over 1817 to 2017. An arithmetical scale would exaggerate any recent changes in value of RPI, as the absolute value of the change is far higher now than a similar proportional change 200 years ago. Conversely, changes in the value of the pound would be exaggerated in the early years of the period, when the value is relatively high. This presentational issue is overcome by using a logarithmic scale, with which equal proportional increases result in the same changes in the vertical axis.

The chart illustrates how the value of the pound, while fluctuating from year to year, was maintained almost constant throughout the Victorian era, and up to the start of the First World War. There was an inflationary spike during and immediately after the First World War, and a steady fall in prices from then almost up to the Second World War. Since the start of the Second World War, inflationary pressures have caused a dramatic fall in the value of the pound year on year.

# Coal Duties

Coal imported into the City, brought by sea to wharves on the river, had been taxed by the City of London since medieval times. By the nineteenth century this 'sea coal' was being augmented by coal brought by canal and later by railway.

    A variety of acts extended the city's authority in collection of duties, fixed the amount of the duty, established the purposes for which the duties were to be utilised, and defined the boundaries of the area over which the duties applied. These were octroi taxes, taxes collected on goods brought into a district for consumption.

**A2.1**: Coal Tax Post alongside 5-furlong post of Epsom Downs Racecourse, erected in 1861. Another Coal Tax Post can be seen on the grassy knoll in the background. (R. Haworth)

The London Coal and Wine Continuance Act 1861 set the final structure until duties were abolished. The Metropolitan Police District, together with the City of London, became the district and many new markers were erected at the boundaries on roads and tracks as well as railways and canals. Altogether some 280 markers were placed, of which over 200 survive. Two examples are illustrated – A2.1 and A2.2. These 'City coal-tax octroi posts' had no connection with wine duties.

The duties were used primarily for rebuilding or new building. In 1670 they provided funds for rebuilding St Paul's Cathedral and fifty-one of the eighty-six churches destroyed in the Great Fire.

From 1767 onwards duties were used inter alia for building Blackfriars Bridge, Holborn Viaduct and the new Coal Exchange.

In 1862 most of the duties were transferred to the Metropolitan Board of Works and directed to a 'Thames Embankment and Metropolis Improvement Fund' used to build the Victoria, Albert and Chelsea Embankments, Hyde Park Corner and other infrastructure including the northern and southern outfall sewers that halted the 'Great Stink'. The City of London received the residual duties, devoting them to improvements at Cannon Street and other City sites.

Railway companies were responsible for collecting the duties on all coal that was brought past the boundary markers and had to make weekly returns of the coal they brought into the district. These returns should provide an important source of information about coal movements but, if the data exists, it has not been found by the author.

Coal duties became an increasingly unpopular tax on an essential commodity, exhibiting both a regressive nature and failing the test of representation, as they impacted those outside the boundaries while benefitting only the metropolis. Two further acts of 1863 and 1868 extended coal duties to 1889, when they were abolished.

**A2.2**: A granite obelisk about 4m high, typical of those put up next to railways. It has the City's shield on its face. (R. Haworth)

# Bibliography and Sources

Allen, Cecil J., *The London & North Eastern Railway*, Ian Allen, 1966.

Anderson, Paul, *The Great British Railway Station: Kings Cross*, Irwell Press, 2016.

Armstrong, William G., 'On the Application of Water Pressure, as a Motive Power, for working Cranes and other descriptions of Machinery', *Proceedings of the Institution of Civil Engineers*, Vol. 9, 1850.

Bawtree, Maurice, 'The City of London Coal Duties and their Boundary Marks', *London Archaeologist*, Spring 1969.

Bradley, Simon, *The Railways: Nation, Network & People*, Profile Books, 2016.

Brown, Jane, *I had a Pitch on the Stones,* Nicholson & Watson, 1946.

Camden History Society, *Streets of St Pancras: Somers Town & the Railway Lands*, 2002.

Campkin, Ben, *Remaking London,* I.B.Tauris, 2013.

Clarke, Linda, *Building Capitalism: Historical Change and the Labour Process in the Production of the Built Environment*, Routledge, 1992.

Coster, Peter J., *The Book of the Great Northern: The Main Line: Part One: Kings Cross to Welwyn Garden City*, Irwell Press, 2010.

Darley, Peter, *Camden Goods Station Through Time,* Amberley Publishing, 2013.

Dawes, Rev. Martin C., *The End of the Line: The Story of the Railway Service to the Great Northern London Cemetery*, Barnet & District Local History Society, 2003.

Denford, Steven L.J., *Agar Town: The Life & Death of a Victorian 'Slum'*, Camden History Society Occasional Paper, 1995.

Dix, Charles, 'Railways and the Growth of Industries: the Egyptian Quail Traffic', *Railway Magazine,* No. 33, 1913.

Duckworth, Stephen P & Barry V. Jones, *King's Cross Development Site: an Inventory of Architectural and Industrial Features*, EHC01/147 A Report for English Heritage, November 1988.

Edensor, Tim, *Industrial Ruins: Space, Aesthetics and Morality*, Oxford: Berg, 2005.

Erwood, Peter, *Memories of King's Cross Goods, 1937/38,* Railways South East, Volume 1, Winter 1988–89.

Faulkner, Alan, *The Regent's Canal,* Waterways World Ltd, 2005.

Firth, J.F.B., *The Coal and Wine Dues: the History of the London Coal Tax and the Arguments For and Against its Renewal,* Municipal Reform Pamphlet No. 20, reprinted from *The Times* of 7 December 1886, The Anti-Coal Tax Committee, 1887.

Gairns, J.F., 'Notable Railway Stations and their Traffic: King's Cross – Great Northern Railway', *Railway Magazine*, August 1914.

Gordon, William John, *The Horse-World of London, Religious Tract Society,* 1893.

Greenwood, James, *In Strange Company, Henry S. King and Co.,*1874.

Grinling, Charles H., *The History of the Great Northern Railway, 1845–95,* Methuen & Co., 1898.

Haslam, Rebecca & Guy Thompson, *An Immense & Exceedingly Commodious Goods Station, Monograph 1,* Pre-Construct Archaeology, 2016.

Hawkins, Chris, *The Great British Railway Station: Kings Cross*, Irwell Press, 1990.

Hayes, David A. & Marian Kamlish, *The King's Cross Fraudster: Leopold Redpath, His Life & Times,* Camden History Society, 2013.

Howeson, Anne, *Remember Me, King's Cross in Transition,* The Guardian and Royal College of Art, 2009 (catalogue of solo exhibition at King's Place).

Howeson, Anne, *Present in the Past: Renovation and Revival in King's Cross Central* (catalogue of solo exhibition at Collyer Bristow Gallery).

Humber, William, 'On the design and arrangement of railway stations, repairing shop, engine sheds', *Proceedings of the Institution of Civil Engineers,* Volume 25, 1866.

Hunter, Michael & Robert Thorne (Eds), *Change at King's Cross,* Historical Publications, 1990.

Inglis, Angela, *Railway Lands,* Matador, 2007.

Inglis, Angela, with Nigel Buckner, *King's Cross: A Sense of Place,* Matador, 2012.

Johns, C.A., 'One Hundred Years at King's Cross', *Railway Magazine*, Part 1 (Oct) & Part 2 (Nov) 1952.

Kay, Peter, 'The First King's Cross: The 1850 GNR Terminus in Maiden Lane and its Subsequent Fate', *London's Industrial Archaeology*, No. 7, GLIAS, 2000.

Kay, Peter, 'The Great Northern Main Line in London: Belle Isle', *The London Railway Record*, April 2007.

King's Cross Railway Lands Group, 'The King's Cross Development – People or Profit?' July 1989.

Lacroix, Eugène (Ed.), *Nouveau portfeuille de l'ingenieur des chemins de fer,* Flachat, Eugène, Auguste Perdonnet & Camille Polonceau, Paris: Librairie Scientifique, Industrielle et Agricole, 1866. ETH – Bibliothek, Zürich, Rar 4631, http://dx.doi.org/10.3931/e-rara-20097/ Public Domain Mark.

Lucas, R.G., 'King's Cross Cemetery Station', *Railway Magazine*, October 1954.

McKenna, Frank, *The Railway Workers 1840–1970,* Faber, 1980.

Mayo, Charles, *Ghosts of Steam,* Sue Elliott, 2012.

Medcalf, J., 'Railway Goods Depots: IV – King's Cross Goods Station', *Railway Magazine*, Vol. 6, April 1900.

Medcalf, J, Early Days, 'King's Cross: A Christmas Reverie', *Railway Magazine,* Vol. 6, 1900.

Norden, John, *Speculum Britanniae: the First Parte: an Historicall, & Chorographicall Discription of Middlesex*, 1593.

Parkes, Michael & Daniel C., Mouawad with King's Cross Railway Lands Group, *Interim Uses Initiative, from Blight to Bloom,* December 1993.

Pinks, William J., *The History of Clerkenwell,* Pickburn, 1865.

Roberts, G.A., 'Remodelling of King's Cross Station', *LNER Magazine,* 28 (11), November 1938.

Rose, John, *Solidarity Forever: 100 years of Kings Cross ASLEF,* Kings Cross ASLEF, 1986.

Russell, Janet, *Great Western Horse Power,* Oxford Publishing, 1995.

Russell, Janet K.L., *G.W.R. Company's Servants,* Wild Swan, 1983.

Simmons, Jack, *The Railway in Town and Country 1830–1914,* David & Charles, 1886.

Survey of London, Vol. 47, *Northern Clerkenwell and Pentonville,* Philip Temple (Ed.), 2008.

Tatlow, Peter, *LNER Wagons,* Pendragon, 1998.

*The Idler,* Issue 36, Winter 2005, pp. 76-89, Random House.

Townend, Peter Norman, *Top Shed,* 2nd Edition, Ian Allen, 1989.

Turton, Keith, *The Early Years of London's Coal Trade,* Railway Archive, No. 13.

Wade, George A., 'The Horse Department of a Railway', *Railway Magazine,* Vol. 8, 1900.

Wade, George A., 'Railway Goods Traffic during the Queen's Reign', *Railway Magazine,* Vol. 7, 1900.

Ward, Laurence, *The London County Council Bomb Damage Maps 1939–45,* Thames & Hudson, 2015.

Weale, John, *London Exhibition in 1851,* 1851.

Wrottesley, John, *The Great Northern Railway, Vol. 1: Origins & Development,* Batsford, 1979.

Wrottesley, John, *The Great Northern Railway, Vol. II: Expansion and Competition,* Batsford, 1979.

Wrottesley, John, *The Great Northern Railway, Vol. III: Twentieth Century to Grouping,* Batsford, 1981.

## SELECTED ARCHIVES, JOURNALS AND OTHER SOURCES CONSULTED

*ASLEF Journal*
British History Online
British Library
Camden History Society, newsletter and journal
Camden Local Studies and Archives Centre
Canal and River Trust
Cats Meat Shop
*Greater London Industrial Archaeology Society Journal*
Great Northern Railway Society
Historic England, London and Swindon
Historic Model Railway Society
Institution of Civil Engineers
Ironbridge Gorge Museum
Islington Local History Centre
King's Cross Railway Lands Group

*King's Cross Voices*
LNER Encyclopedia Discussion Forum
London Metropolitan Archives
*London Railway Record*
Model Railway Club
Museum of London
National Archives
National Railway Museum
Network Rail Record Centre
Parliamentary Archives
Railway and Canal Historical Society
Royal Collection, Windsor Castle
Royal Institute of British Architects
Royal Veterinary College
Victoria and Albert Museum
Wellcome Library

A gas street light, Goods Way, *c*.1955, John
Gay. (Historic England)

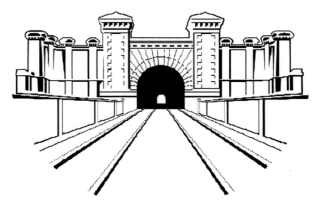

CAMDEN
RAILWAY HERITAGE
TRUST

The History Press

The destination for history
www.thehistorypress.co.uk